Legal Challenges to Behavior Modification

Trends in Schools, Corrections and Mental Health

Reed Martin

Research Press / 2612 North Mattis Avenue / Champaign, Illinois 61820

ISBN 0-87822-158-1

To Judy
who constantly challenged me to write a better book

Foreword

Modifying behavior is the business of many of our public institutions, most notably schools, corrections, and mental health programs. The clients of these institutions and the general public want such benefits of "behavior modification" as education, rehabilitation, and training for success in society. But the techniques used, and the procedures through which they are offered, are the source of increasing legal problems.

Because of rapid changes, and many cases still on appeal, this book will focus on *trends* in the law. It is aimed at an audience of practitioners of behavior change and administrators of such programs in public institutions. Consequently, the organization of the book reflects the planning and implementation of a behavior change program rather than being grouped around legal doctrines.

Hopefully, others may profit from this book. Any potential client, or a friend or attorney counseling that client, will be challenged to raise many questions about a proposed program—not to defeat efforts at treatment, but rather to make it the very best possible.

Contents

1

The Growing Legal Challenge

SUMMARY

The law and the behavioral sciences are not necessarily antagonistic to each other. Many of the recent changes in the law, e.g. requirements that schools educate all handicapped children, occurred because the behavioral sciences demonstrated that it was possible for government agencies to do a better job. And many new pressures on public institutions caused by changes in the law will be best satisfied by a behavioral approach (i.e. concrete goals, measurable progress, objective results).

But there is a growing legal challenge to *all* public programs as courts begin to inquire into areas previously left to administrative discretion. Clients of public services are protected by the Constitution against practitioners of behavior change employed by government agencies. That protection is being applied in judicial interpretations of the Constitution and in new administrative guidelines which govern many behavior change programs. This chapter describes the basic sources of law relied on in current legal controversies and the general trend established in eight key cases recently decided.

HANDS OFF

After years of observing a "hands off" policy,[1] courts have begun to probe inside schools, prisons, and mental health programs. The resulting judicial decisions will profoundly affect the way behavior change can be attempted in our public institutions.

Courts previously did not inquire into social service activities for several reasons. Such activities were considered executive branch functions, and courts felt they should not attempt to substitute their judgment for that of the "experts" running the institution. But most significant, the courts sided with the administrators because the clients—prisoners, the mentally infirm, or children—were considered to have no rights to assert against the institution.[2] Today's far-reaching legal challenges began to occur as these clients were perceived to have rights.

SOURCES OF LEGAL POLICY

Due Process

The substance of those rights has been sketched in over the past decade, mainly on the basis of the notion of fair play espoused in the Constitution's due process clause.[3] That clause provides that if government activity affects a citizen in a way that would deprive him of liberty or property, it must do so with due process of law. Courts first began to rule that due process required notice of what behavior was prohibited—that is, what would get a person in trouble. This element of due process began to curtail the wide discretion administrators had been accustomed to. Now, for example, school administrators would have to specify in writing the offenses for which a student could be disciplined, and the specifications had to be clear: no more "conduct unbecoming a student" or "insubordination." Individuals must also be notified that the rule is going to be applied because some offense is suspected.

Once a rule was established and was going to be applied to an individual, courts ruled that fair play required a hearing to determine the merits of the charge. Different courts have allowed wide latitude in determining what a hearing must entail, but it basically involves allowing the affected party the opportunity to defend himself. At first, courts were reluctant to require that the hearing be very elaborate. The institution was assumed to be acting in the client's best interest, and a full hearing—with lawyers and cross-examination of witnesses—would seem to admit that there was an adversary process. But courts have realized it *is* adversary when a prison

2

administrator considers putting a prisoner in isolation, or when a mental institution considers using an aversive therapy, or when a school plans to expel a student. Thus hearings are generally required to be held before an impartial entity, with an opportunity to hear witnesses, with the individual represented by counsel, and with an opportunity to appeal.[4]

The emergence of these due process rights challenges a basic assumption of many behavior change specialists who work in public institutions. They feel that they are experts working on behalf of their clients and that they should therefore be allowed wide discretion. But to the degree that their behavior change approach restricts a client, they have to follow specific rules and be able to justify their decision in a hearing.

Equal Protection

A second major source of law which has extended rights to clients of social services is the Constitution's equal protection clause.[5] That clause provides that citizens cannot be denied the equal protection of the law—in other words, a state agency cannot treat one group substantially differently from other groups entitled to the same treatment. For example, a school cannot simply refuse to deal with handicapped children.

The significance for the behavior change practitioner is that his program cannot single out one group for a specific type of treatment without being able to justify making the distinction. If a school behavior modification project seeking to deal with disruptive students only treats blacks, or boys, or a certain socio-economic class, then it may well be denying the equal protection of the law. It may provide good therapy and a needed program, but it must be reorganized if it is to continue.

Judicial Decisions: Important Precedents

The third major source of law is the common law—court cases which build legal doctrines precedent by precedent. Several recent cases must be understood by those seeking to work in the field of behavior change. As mentioned earlier, our interest is not the specific rule of law as it exists at this writing, but the likely trend of the law and the way in which decisions will be used for precedents.

Living conditions. One of the most widely publicized recent cases is *Clonce v. Richardson,*[6] which involved the START (Special Training and Rehabilitative Treatment) program at the federal prison psychiatric facility in Springfield, Missouri. Prisoners denoted as troublemakers were transferred into the program involuntarily. Everyone started in a bare cell and "earned" back basic amenities. The court held that since the change in status involved a deprivation of liberty and property, each prisoner had a right to a hearing in which he could challenge the transfer.

In *Wyatt v. Stickney,* Alabama facilities for the mentally ill and retarded were found to be below the minimum level at which adequate treatment could occur. The court detailed certain minimum rights—clothing, food, a comfortable bed, privacy, and so forth. These are constitutionally protected rights and not privileges: They must be provided. Individuals cannot be forced to earn them as in *Clonce.*

Right to treatment or release. Donaldson v. O'Connor established that, in addition to minimum living conditions, there is a right to either treatment or release. Donaldson was virtually left to his own devices, wandering among other mental patients for fifteen years. The court held that the only justification for confinement was treatment, and that if some treatment was not forthcoming, the patient must be released.[7]

Not only must there be treatment, but *Wyatt* and *Donaldson* influenced the court in *Morales v. Turman* to require higher standards of individual treatment, including periodic reviews of progress. In that case, the Texas juvenile justice system was found to be not providing treatment as constitutionally required.

Does the institution's duty to treat mean it can carry out any treatment it wants? In *Kaimowitz v. Michigan Department of Mental Health,* the court argued that a confined patient was inherently coerced, and that the hospital could not conduct therapy (in this case, psychosurgery) that was experimental and that therefore required consent. Consent is becoming a more important element in much judicial thinking, and courts will look at all the conditions to determine whether consent is really informed and voluntary.

Least restrictive alternative. In *Lake v. Cameron* an elderly, senile woman was involuntarily confined to a mental institution, and the court ordered that the institution explore other less restrictive alternatives. Coupled with other cases, this decision suggests that when a behavior change program is undertaken, its proponent must show why any less restrictive approaches would not be worth pursuing. This would seem an impossibly heavy burden for any approach proposing institutionalization or other confinement in order to totally control the environment.

Duty to provide services. If, when treatment must be provided, it cannot be coerced and must be the least restrictive alternative, it seems that practitioners would be tempted to simply ignore the really tough cases. But the *Pennsylvania Association for Retarded Children* case established that services must be offered to all those entitled to receive them. So, for example, severely retarded children can no longer be ignored by the public schools; they must instead be treated, with an ultimate goal of raising the level of functioning to allow each child to enter the mainstream of education.

This mainstream cannot itself become a *de facto* exclusion from service by simply throwing everyone together and not treating the more difficult cases. In *New York State Association for Retarded Children v. Rockefeller* the court found clients whose condition was worsening after being involved with the state's program. This has profound significance for behavior change research: Not only must the therapy not worsen the client's condition, but persons cannot be placed in control groups and allowed to worsen for lack of treatment.

Liability. When problems do arise because client rights have not been fulfilled, behavior change practitioners might be held personally responsible. In *Donaldson* the psychiatrists in charge were assessed $38,500 personally in damages. In a recently filed case,[8] the court will be asked to find the supervisors of the state's mental health program negligent for failure to set up a system that works. The trend is for those in charge to be held to a duty to find out when something goes wrong and to make it right.

And the practitioner will not be allowed all the time he wants. The courts in *Wyatt* and other cases are requiring a periodic review of progress; if there is no progress, the program might very well be terminated.

Thus the third source of law—judicial decisions—is very much in flux and is constantly growing. Basically, a behavior change program must meet certain minimum standards of care; an individual must be able to challenge his inclusion in the project; the subject must be treated with an individual program; coercion will be subject to challenge; the least restrictive treatment alternative is to be explored first; if periodic reviews of progress show no change, the program may be terminated; and if the subject's condition worsens, the person in charge may be held liable.

Administrative Guidelines

A fourth area providing a rich new source of law for courts to apply is administrative guidelines. As the federal government's involvement in the behavior change area has grown, funding sources such as the Department of Health, Education and Welfare have issued extensive regulations on such topics as consent in experimental treatment. Behavior change practitioners receiving funds from any governmental entity must follow the applicable guidelines[9] or else face a hard battle if ever taken to court.

ANTI-BEHAVIOR MOD?

When all of these sources of law are taken together, some behavior change practitioners argue that there is a conscious effort to outlaw their field of practice. Otherwise, they argue, why would there be so many recent lawsuits aimed at behavior change projects?

There are several answers. First, the lawsuits have been directed at ineffective or harmful institutions. To the degree that behavioral programs are an integral part of those institutions, they will share the attack. Very few behavior modification programs have been singled out for attack, and I have not read any decision adverse to a behavioral program which did not deserve to be questioned or curtailed.

The second reason for these lawsuits is that there are real complaints, real people actually being affected. Many behavior change practitioners like to discuss the field as if it were theoretical, and they view the classroom or professional journals as the preferred forum for debate. But when an individual claims injury, the appropriate forum is a court. Recent legal challenges reflect the nature of our increasingly litigious society, not a plot to stop behavior modification. Practitioners of psychosurgery, electrical stimulation of the brain, electroconvulsive therapy, drug experimentation, and so forth also feel they are the especial target of the growing legal challenge.

BEHAVIORISM AND CIVIL LIBERTY

Behavior therapists have often expressed a feeling of irony that lawsuits are being brought by civil libertarians wanting to free clients from restraints. The irony, they argue, is that behavior therapy programs intend to free clients from restraints. There are many points common to both behavior therapy and a civil liberties approach—dealing only with overt behavior, discarding the myth of mental illness, looking into the environment rather than into the individual to find solutions to causes of sociopathic behavior, and a desire to help the individual in the least restrictive environment available.

In fact, work in the behavioral field has provided needed scientific evidence to support civil libertarian positions. For many years, it appeared that retarded citizens could not be helped. Consequently, schools were allowed to exclude them, and institutions were not required to provide anything more than custodial care. Analysis of the results of carefully

7

applied behavior change strategies has shown that there is hope for the handicapped when offered proper treatment, [10] and the law now requires much more of our institutions. In another example of similar goals, civil libertarians opposed to corporal punishment in schools cite the more effective discipline available in behavioral classroom management.[11] Unfortunately there are tendencies evidenced by some behaviorists which seem to run counter to the above notions and raise clients', and others', suspicions.

The first tendency is to ignore the fact that many programs are carried out by government institutions. No one likes to think of himself as "the state," especially since many behavior modifiers work only part-time or as consultants in government programs. But to the degree that "the state" is involved in the program, behavior modifiers must admit to attendant legal restraints and not act as if they are private practitioners.

A second tendency is the desire to help everyone with whom they come into contact. This basically good impulse stems from excitement over working with a therapy that seems to produce results. A "helping professional" who develops a skill that actually helps is, understandably, hard to hold down. But the public does not want the state, or behavior therapists working on behalf of the state, enthusiastically involving everyone in a big research and treatment program. If the public perceives such research and experimentation as behavior therapy's goal, there will likely be a backlash, in terms of public regulation, and an increase in legal challenges.

Children's Rights

A final area of recent legal development, which might pit civil liberties lawyers against behavior modifiers, concerns children—the subject of many behavior change efforts. A counselor seeking to deal with a child might be expected to gain the consent of parent or guardian. However, some counselors (particularly school personnel) are beginning to call for a right to help children despite their parents. There are several arguments in favor of this notion. Children are people, and they should be entitled to needed treatment. If a parent-child conflict is the source of a child's problems, the parent might block assistance. Where the problem is one that would likely infuriate a parent—drugs, sex, or a recent abortion—some counselors feel it would only worsen the situation to have to inform the parent before helping the child.

A child should have a right to receive help; but in enforcing that right, care must be taken that the overall interests of the child are not injured.

In several current court cases, state welfare agencies have taken children away from their parents to seek what the state agent felt was needed for the child. In one type of case,[12] parents have decided to let a severely malformed infant die after birth by refusing life-supporting surgery. Efforts have been made by social welfare agencies to gain custody of such children so that they could consent to the surgery. The court decisions have been mixed, but whatever becomes the rule will affect the relation between counselors and children.

In the second type of case,[13] children are taken away from their natural parents for reasons such as that the children were not, in the eyes of some state employee, receiving sufficient intellectual stimulation. In New York, the Bureau of Child Welfare will not admit children to residential treatment services unless the parents relinquish custody. In that state alone, five thousand children of the poor (the affluent can usually afford treatment for their children and need not face that choice) have been taken from their families.[14]

Some behavior change practitioners feel that they know what is best for children, and they might welcome the opportunity to relocate children in new environments. Child counselors in general, frustrated by unresponsive parents, might wish they could just take the child away. But the "right" of state agents to decide that they can do a better job of child raising, that they have rights, on behalf of the child, superior to the parent, is a dangerous trend. It is one being challenged by civil liberties lawyers in several states. Behavior change practitioners would be well-served to direct their efforts toward improving services to parents at home so that families can be kept together and children's interests can be served—and so that another area of legal conflict can be avoided.

THE CHALLENGES WILL CONTINUE
The resolution of any legal challenge to the particular actions of a mental health professional will not always come in a courtroom with a clear and final judgment occurring at the end. The challenge will come in many forums—in the institution, in legislative bodies, in funding or in administration of programs, and in new guidelines. Even after a decision in a particular case, the problem is not over, because implementing a judgment as it applies to clients and staff will require institutional changes, staff retraining, and continuing attention to legal developments.

So the legal challenge is here—and it is going to be with us in the future. It is now very much a part of the life of anyone who cares enough to enter the helping professions to try to change the behavior of another person.

CHAPTER 1 REVIEW CHECKLIST

1. Are the rules under which you operate written down in objective terms?

2. Are the individuals to be affected by a program given notice and an opportunity for a hearing?

3. Is the affected individual allowed the resources needed to challenge inclusion in the program if he wishes to do so?

4. Does the impact of inclusion in the program mean one group of individuals will be treated so differently from others that the distinction cannot be justified?

5. Does the participant in the program receive in services the same types of things which the institution generally provides, or does this program deprive the participants

of something? If the latter, is it a constitutionally protected right or a privilege that is being withheld?

6. Is there an individual treatment program?

7. Are there periodic reviews of progress?

8. Is the least restrictive alternative explored first?

9. Are all the individuals in need of this program being offered services? If some are being excluded, can their separation be justified?

10. Is anyone's condition worsening?

11. Is anyone not receiving help because he has been assigned to a "control" group?

12. Is there a system in operation which allows those in charge to determine if something is going wrong?

13. Have all funding agency guidelines been examined to determine if there are additional requirements?

2

The Decision to Intervene

SUMMARY

Intervening in someone's life to change his behavior is a potential deprivation of liberty sufficient to raise constitutional issues. Such intervention should be limited to behavior which is within the legitimate interest of the institution involved and which actually occurs and is intolerable. Any decision to change behavior must be examined to determine if its impact denies the constitutionally required equal protection of the law. This chapter describes the questions that can be raised about the legitimacy of government interest, the existence of the behavior, the record documenting the behavior, and the decision that the documented behavior is intolerable.

A DEPRIVATION OF LIBERTY

Changing the behavior of another individual may involve a deprivation of liberty which the Constitution says shall not be attempted without due process of law. In many cases the subject of a behavior change program will be physically confined—this is certainly a deprivation of liberty. But recent decisions suggest that the stigma that attaches to psychological treatment and even the change in status that comes with assignment to a special program affect liberty—specifically the ability to associate freely with others—sufficiently to raise the constitutional issue.[1]

The abridgement of freedom which behavior change represents must be justified in terms of a legitimate state interest in the behavior to be changed.[2] No publicly funded program can be allowed to attempt to change every behavior it wishes. Each agency has legitimate spheres of interest and should have specific goals limited to them.

ACTUAL BEHAVIOR: OVERT AND VERIFIABLE

If the behavior to be dealt with falls within the area of legitimate interest of the institution involved, the next area of inquiry should be whether the behavior actually exists. The easiest way to assure this is to deal only with overt, objectively verifiable behavior. This sounds simple and also relatively compatible with the practice of behavior therapy, but a surprising number of behavior change programs attempt to treat individuals who have not committed any specific act that justifies the intervention.

In some behavior programs, intervention is taken as a fact of life. Many mental health professionals in schools, clinics, and prisons are in day-to-day interaction with their clients. They might argue that this constant contact will have an impact on behavior and that the question therefore is not *whether* to intervene, but for what purpose. It is understandable that the therapist would concentrate on "Now that we have him, what do we do with him?" But the law will focus on "Why do you have him in the first place?"

There is good therapeutic justification for this legal focus, because if there were not a specific overt behavior that first directed attention to the individual, there could be no realistic setting of goals. Without goals (see Chapter 5) there can be no real treatment. And since treatment is the justification for the behavior change intervention, the whole basis for interaction with the individual would be on tenuous ground.

Someone Else's Behavior

Social workers and domestic relations court staff are constantly faced with young children in families where parents neglect them. In some states these "children in need of supervision" number in the thousands.[3] No overt behavior of the child has warranted this scrutiny; it is the behavior of the parent which caused the government to intervene. The duty to care for such children, to assume custody of them, and even to place them in foster homes can be carried out without any justification for behavior change. Such children should not find themselves in behavior change programs, because *someone else's behavior* prompted state intervention.[4]

Screening: Predicted Behavior

Predicted behavior also triggers some programs. The frequency of occurrence of actual behavior is usually the baseline for any behavioral intervention, so this should be an implicit methodological safeguard against getting involved with anticipated behavior. But some persons argue for programs that screen for future behavior rather than assessing actual behavior. Dr. Arnold Hutschnecker, a New York physician-turned-psychiatrist, gained prominence when it was revealed he had treated New York lawyer Richard Nixon. The Department of Health, Education and Welfare received a proposal from Hutschnecker suggesting that all six- to eight-year-olds be screened for pre-criminal behavior.[5] Those that flunked the predictive tests were to be sent off to corrective camps run by the federal government. HEW dropped consideration of the plan after some unflattering publicity and the threat of a Congressional inquiry, but it raises the issue: What could possibly be treated before a problem behavior actually occurs?

Some behavior modifiers lean toward the notion of early intervention, thinking that if they could only get to children early enough, they could really help them. Recent federal legislation provides for screening of children prior to school age.[6] To the degree that physical handicaps can be diagnosed and treated, the child can enter first grade ready to go. But what of psychological problems? Will the problems of a three-year-old be similar to the problems that same child will face at twice its age upon entering the new environment of a school? If a child seems "hyperactive" at three, is there therapeutic sense in changing something now, rather than appraising the problem when it actually occurs at the first grade; and is there any legal sense in government intervention at this time? Voluntary programs are in order and are to be

15

commended, but to the degree that government involvement is required in either screening or treatment, then programs must stand on much firmer ground than a statistical prediction of behavior.

Perhaps the most extreme case of screening involves genetic screening prior to birth. The assumption is that many physical abnormalities and behavior, particularly socially intolerable behavior such as uncontrollable aggression, are linked to genes.[7] Some geneticists theorize that if they could remedy what they perceive to be genetic defects, they could prevent such behavior from occurring at a later date. The law should certainly not tolerate such meddling in the absence of an actually existing behavior.

Functional Deficits: Absence of an Overt Behavior

Our discussion of what justifies a government interest has focused on actual observable behavior. Of equal interest in many behavior change programs are functional deficits—needed behavior that one does *not* perform. As discussed before, the main problem is whether the behavior to be taught is within the legitimate interest of the government agency in question. If it is, then the problems in creating new behavior are far less than in suppressing an existing behavior.

DOCUMENTING BEHAVIOR

Whether the behavior is an intolerable excess or a functional deficit, its existence must be documented. The most typical documentation would be found in some kind of past history of the individual. Such histories are often composed of assorted anecdotes, observations, and test results.

Interviews and Observations

The immediate question to raise is how much of your decision to treat will be based on information from others. Such secondhand information has no protection against bias. Anecdotes from a teacher wanting a student to be sent to a

16

special program, or from a parent wanting a family member to be committed, may not tell the whole story and may be susceptible to legal challenges.

Obviously the best record is the one that can be compiled by observing and talking to the individual. This would be most reliable if the prospective client were still in his natural environment and the behavior occurred with some frequency. Often, however, the person has been removed from that environment and installed in a new institutional setting. The danger then is that you may be observing, and deciding to treat, a different behavior than that which first precipitated the desire to treat.

Testing as Documentation

Authority to test. These problems of subjectivity and reliability[8] are often dealt with by resorting to tests. But there should be some prior and legitimate reason to give the test, such as an overt behavior which is in the purview of the government agency. Many who have surveyed recent student rights developments as they apply to school psychology have predicted that the next area will be "the right to be let alone."[9] Several school systems have recently outlawed IQ tests,[10] and there is a general rebellion against tests which seem either to screen for possible problems or which probe areas of questionable relevance. [11]

Thus the authority to test might be challenged. The most persuasive justification would be that a specific overt behavior indicated a need for testing. If that judgment can be sustained, the next challenge will likely be to the type of test chosen.

Selecting a test. Cultural bias exists in some tests to the extent that a culturally different person's answers will appear to be wrong. IQ tests have been the source of much litigation charging that minority-culture students have been wrongly diagnosed as being in need of special programs.[12] Language bias is also common. If the language used is not the person's native language or is above his education level, then the test may produce inaccurate results. In one recent example, large numbers of Spanish-speaking children were classified as retarded and placed in special programs on the basis of a test administered in English. When a court ordered retesting in Spanish, the vast majority scored in the normal range.[13]

Administering the test. If there is authority to test, and the test selected is appropriate, there may be a challenge to the conditions under which it is administered. Some persons, particularly mental patients, may be put on drugs as soon as they enter an institution. Others may receive shock treatment early in their confinement. If testing occurs while the client is tranquilized or disoriented from shock treatments, then you might well expect a later challenge that the testing was fatally flawed. Such a challenge might succeed in expunging from the record all observations noted during that period to avoid the risk that they might later serve as the basis for a treatment classification.

Test interpretation. If test administration is satisfactory, the next challenge may be to interpretation. To the degree that the test produces subjective data, such as personality traits assumed to be projected in responses to ambiguous stimuli, the interpretation will be highly subject to personal bias and error. The legal yardstick to be applied focuses on the standard of care and expertise practiced by the psychological profession. The counselor is not expected to be perfect or even right, but he is charged with the duty to keep up with the standards of his profession. How that is determined may be the subject of professional discipline committees, but it is also the subject of legal challenges and judicial inquiries. There is the question whether a single school psychologist could be the determinant of a classification decision. Some recent trends suggest that such decisions should be made by a team of psychologists; perhaps the decision of even a person meeting the highest standards of his profession is not enough, if he acts alone.

A related concern in interpretation of the record is whether it will aid in prescribing treatment. A description of the behavior in non-behavioral terms may serve little purpose. Some catchall phrase such as "minimal brain dysfunction," "hyperactive," or "schizophrenic" is of little prescriptive use. It does not put the individual on notice of what the problem behavior is, and it does not aid the counselor in setting goals. It therefore increases the likelihood that the individual will get nonspecific aid. Legal rights and requirements can better be served by the use of behaviorally specific descriptions.

IS THE BEHAVIOR INTOLERABLE?

Even if the behavior lies within the institution's legitimate interest, and documentation can be offered that the behavior occurred, a program of behavior change should not be implemented unless the behavior is intolerable. If it can be tolerated and ignored, it certainly does not justify intervention. (A behaviorist might argue that "ignoring" is one of the techniques of behavior modification so that whether one pays attention or ignores, there will be an impact. But we are talking about justification for a *program* of treatment, and if ignoring is all that is needed then there would seem to be no program as such.)

Several years ago at Washington, D.C. National Airport, a visitor from England waiting for a change in planes felt she could best occupy her time by emptying some of the many filled ashtrays in the main waiting room. Any frequent visitor to that facility would certainly wish her well, but an airport policeman decided on the spot that she was crazy and had her committed to a local mental institution. In a Washington suburb in Northern Virginia, a retired army officer was awakened in the middle of the night by a loud party. He dressed hastily and went across the street to the police substation to protest. He was quite irritated and was on medication which happened to slur his speech. The police observed his odd dress, his slurred speech, and his excitement, and promptly had him committed. In both instances the individuals were released after legal action was begun.[14] Had they been retained, would some therapist have attempted to change their behavior? The behavior which brought them to the attention of the government did not warrant confinement, and it would not have provided a goal for behavior

19

change. A program begun on the basis of overt behavior that is clearly not intolerable would be legally and therapeutically flawed.

Intolerable to Whom?

Others, particularly juveniles, become the focus of behavior change efforts after overt behavior that is pronounced intolerable, but the question must be asked: "Intolerable to whom?" Some in positions of authority will denote behavior as intolerable, and thus in need of change, because of sex bias, age discrimination, and intolerance to certain lifestyles.[15]

Sex bias leads to many faulty treatment decisions.[16] Some conduct is considered intolerable only when engaged in by girls; but if it would be tolerated in a boy, it should be ignored in both. Sex role discrimination by professionals also influences decisions. In some mental institutions, if a woman complains about housework, that may be one behavior selected for change. If a man complained about having to do so much housework, the majority of counselors would probably consider that complaint normal, certainly not a problem to be treated.

Similarly, juveniles find themselves the subject of treatment for conduct which would be ignored if they were a few months older. A seventeen-year-old who refuses to do what his parents say might be considered incorrigible (hardly an offense in the adult world), institutionalized, and selected for a behavior change program. A few months later, the young person would not be classified as in need of treatment. So age-related legal judgments should not override professional judgments about who actually needs treatment and for what. A behavioral counselor in a state home for delinquent girls in Louisiana reported that when the "offense" was running away from home (an age-related offense) and where the facts indicated the home was absolutely intolerable, she considered the behavior normal and not a subject for treatment.

Lifestyle bias is another cause of a judgment by authorities that conduct is intolerable and must be changed.

Some schools try to discipline students in regard to hair length, dress, speech, and other aspects of personal behavior. Many courts, including the Supreme Court, have severely limited schools' discretion and afforded constitutional protection for many areas of personal expression.[17] But even in areas not yet specifically dealt with, the question should be raised as to whether the complaint about the behavior really only reflects an intolerance for a youthful lifestyle. If so, the professional who begins a program of behavior change under those circumstances may meet a legal challenge.

Prevention of Intolerable Behavior

Some persons become candidates for behavior change efforts after an overt behavior which in itself does not justify intervention but which appears to the counselor to be the beginning of a series of increasingly intolerable behaviors. The seemingly humane justification for intervention now is to prevent worse trouble later. Statistically we can draw a simple progression in school: poor academic performance, truancy, running away from home, and then committing a crime to get money. When a counselor is confronted with the first components of this progression, may he presume to treat for all of them or to begin treatment at all? If a mental patient begins to refuse to cooperate or a prisoner begins swearing at guards, is there a need to begin to change behavior? Such preventive approaches have several possible flaws.

One problem occurs if the initial behavior in the presumed continuum is too slight to justify intervention in the first place. A number of research projects have attempted to analyze "pre-delinquency" and catch it at its earliest sign.[18] Consequently such projects focus on smaller and smaller behaviors. One list drawn up by a social worker in North Carolina listed nailbiting as a pre-delinquent indicator. The actual overt behavior which initially brings the intervention of the state must be both serious enough to justify the state action and related to a legitimate government interest.

A second problem with preventive approaches is that once the individual's behavior is seen as justifying intervention, the result may be a "total" program which deals with dozens of behaviors. The initial behavior may be forgotten while other behaviors are shaped. Or equally bad, the individual might be kept in the total program long after the initial behavior is successfully changed.

There is an understandable desire to deal with the whole child, the whole environment, and a whole range of behaviors. But the program is on shaky ground if it seeks to treat for more than really happened or to change behaviors that are not that serious.

Predicting Intolerable Behavior

Some instances of overt behavior which are definitely not socially acceptable could still be tolerated if there were no reason to believe that they would occur again. But this involves the questionable practice of predicting behavior. Even if behavior, in general, seems predictably responsive to certain stimuli that does not mean a *specific* behavior, such as suicide or assault, can be predicted with certainty; in fact, attempts to predict dangerous behavior fall statistically below the average that could be achieved by flipping a coin.[19]

A single instance of problem behavior may justify intervention to work on the recurring problem behaviors which comprise the larger act. But a prediction of repetition of the larger problem behavior cannot be the justification for the intervention because there can be no real treatment. With no recurring overt behavior—only a predicted one—the practitioner cannot set goals, devise a plan, measure progress, or determine eligibility for release from the program. The result will be no specific treatment and indefinite retention in the program.

What Is "Intolerable"?

To remove the notion of "intolerable" from the realm of subjectivity, each institution must formulate written rules which describe behaviors that cannot be ignored and which, in its view, justify intervention. Written rules will provide an opportunity for challenge and will put individuals on notice of proscribed activity. Such rules, along with documentation of occurrences of behavior, will form the basis of hearings to challenge proposed action. Only then will the requirements of due process be met in regard to decisions to intervene.

EQUAL PROTECTION

Even if due process is satisfied, the behavior change effort might fail if its impact denies equal protection as guaranteed in the Constitution. Schools often place students in "tracks" according to perceived academic ability. Students in a slower track might become targets for a behavior change effort. From an educational perspective this classification might make sense, but if all the students in the slow track happen to be black, or Spanish-speaking, or male, then the argument can be expected that they are being denied equal treatment.[20] In San Francisco an "alternative school" was established to which troublesome students were sent for behavior change. Its population was almost all black: White discipline problems were dealt with in one way, blacks in another.[21] In some schools, white students functioning poorly are called "learning disabled," while blacks receive the harsher designation "educably mentally retarded."[22] In many school systems truants picked up by legal authorities are sent into a correctional process that may include behavior change. When middle-class and upper-class students are truant, the school often calls their homes, but when poorer students are truant, the authorities may be called. Equal treatment?

Thus if you can determine that your decisions to intervene fall into a pattern the impact of which is a different treatment for one discernible group, you should correct it.

Deciding who to include in a behavior change program is also deciding who to exclude. There are legal constraints on the decision *not* to treat as well as on the decision to intervene.[23] Your activity cannot exclude a discernible class of individuals without a justifiable reason for treating them differently.

If your program can meet the legal requirements of due

process and equal protection in deciding when and with whom to intervene to change behavior, you must then face the next step—securing consent.

CHAPTER 2 REVIEW CHECKLIST

1. Does your institution have a legitimate interest in the behavior which you are focusing on?

2. Is the behavior actually occurring (or if a functional deficit, is it failing to occur) regularly enough to justify intervention?

3. Can it be documented objectively enough to withstand the scrutiny of an impartial hearing officer or even a judge?

4. If that documentation includes test data, was there a right to administer the test, was the choice of test reasonably free of bias, were the conditions under which the test was administered acceptable, and can the interpretation of test results withstand objective scrutiny?

5. Does the institution have written down what behaviors it feels would justify intervention?

6. Are such judgments of what is intolerable free of bias about sex, age, race, or style of conduct?

7. Does the behavior which brought the individual to the attention of the institution justify intervention in itself, or is it only the beginning of a presumed continuum of worse behaviors?

3

Consent

SUMMARY

The first step in any behavior change program is to gain consent. There should be consent to the government contact which forms the basis for a judgment about a program, and the individual should be notified that information is being gathered. Once a program is contemplated, the standards for consent may vary depending upon how experimental the approach may be; but basically, consent requires capacity to understand, voluntariness, and notice of the risks and benefits of the proposed program. This chapter describes how to determine at what point the consent process must begin and details the basic elements of consent.

WHEN SHOULD CONSENT BEGIN:
LIMITS ON GOVERNMENT INTERVENTION

Gaining access to an individual for the purposes of behavior change intervention may take various forms. A school teacher or counselor may be required to work with the student. A psychologist in a hospital may have all his clients thrust upon him. But in some cases, the counselor and prospective client may not just happen to be in each other's environment. Gaining access under those conditions poses a different type of problem—whether you have a right to be there and to obtain information without first obtaining the client's consent.

In private cases, professional ethics about soliciting business probably suffice. But where the counselor involves a government agency there is a unique threat, for a potential client can unwittingly be ensnared in a therapeutic environment. For example, when police answer a "family fight" call

25

in Boston they may check back later for counseling.[1] If you drink while driving in Seattle, you may face a series of counseling sessions.[2] If you are in public housing in Washington, D.C. and your children are nuisances, you may have to go into counseling.[3] All these might be good initially: It would be great to prevent family fights or drunken driving; and helping a troublesome child in a housing project now might save him and others much grief later.

But caution must be observed in granting to state agents an access to individuals which creates information that may form the basis for psychological treatment. The best consensual safeguard would be a type of warning that the person is being observed or that information is being solicited for the purpose of making such a judgment. In criminal law, the Fourth Amendment[4] provides limits on physical searches and seizures. If state agents plan to intervene, they must first name the specific thing to be searched for and cannot seize beyond those bounds. If they do, whatever they might discover cannot be used in a proceeding against the individual.

Should Counselors Give Warning?

Every television viewer is familiar with the admonition to a suspect, "You have the right to remain silent. Anything you say may be used against you." A similar warning may be called for in psychological counseling. One recent Supreme Court case[5] suggested a constitutional right to refuse to cooperate with a psychiatrist trying to get information from an individual. There may well be an enforceable right to be put on notice that the state is now trying to get information that will form the basis for some action in regard to the individual. Thus as soon as the practitioner decides he wants to get information that might form the basis for including an individual in a program, such as the documentation described in Chapter 2, he should gain consent.

Treatment, Research, or Experiment?

The consent secured will differ on the basis of what the practitioner has in mind. A program which involves well-tested and accepted procedures might require little consent. For example, if a teacher has been attempting to motivate his children in one widely accepted way and decides to switch over to a different, but also widely accepted, way of structuring the classroom environment to gain more motivation, he is unlikely to need anyone's consent.

If there is an element of research in the program, with pre-program baseline data, information gathered during the program, evaluation, follow-up data collection, and even some publication, then more consent is needed. And consent should be obtained for each discrete step in the process. A person consenting to participate in a program of treatment is not necessarily consenting to eventual publication of the results.

The question whether a program is experimental is hard to determine in advance. If your approach is not widely reported and well accepted in the professional literature, if there are risks (particularly physical risks to the individuals involved), or if the risk:benefit ratio is small, the approach is probably experimental. A court would apply the highest requirements for consent in such a case.

REQUIREMENTS ON CONSENT

Those requirements should be spelled out in great detail in written regulations under which the particular agency operates. In addition, any funding agency will probably have requirements on consent of persons in programs paid for with their funds. Such guidelines[6] vary from agency to agency, and federal guidelines are still in flux. The recently created National Commission for the Protection of Human Subjects of Biomedical and Behavioral Research[7] will recommend further guidelines for behavioral activity. But all guidelines are at best only minimum requirements, and any program would hopefully strive to gain the fullest possible consent.

Capacity to Consent

The first requirement is the client's capacity to consent. "Capacity" implies a sound mind and sufficient age to be able to act on one's own behalf. Thus, children, some mental patients and some "disturbed" prisoners may be presumed not to have the capacity to consent. Even though capacity is presumably lacking in children, there is a current trend to secure their "consent" when they are to be involved. This does not really alter anything from a legal standpoint, nor does it preclude the necessity for parental consent, but it seems to have a valuable therapeutic basis and seems admirable from a human viewpoint. The same should be true of those presumed retarded or incompetent.

If the potential client does not have the capacity to consent, then the consent of a parent or guardian may be secured. That currently meets legal requirements, but it does not necessarily safeguard client rights and can be expected to be attacked in the future. The problem is that in the case of a mental patient, the parent or guardian is most likely the person who brought the client into contact with the counselor in the first place; that parent or guardian is certainly likely to consent to the proposed therapy. In the case of students, parents are likely to go along with the recommendation of the school professional. The law is willing to accept this at present because it assumes the child does not have the capacity to protest and that the parent or guardian always acts in the student's best interests.[8] The parent or guardian does not have the power, however, to consent to some treatment which is illegal or which poses unnecessary risk to the client, and these limitations are likely to be extended in the future.

If the person is in the custody of an institution, and does not have capacity, the institution might consent on his behalf. This really means there are no client safeguards—the very institution which proposes the treatment is also consenting to it! This seemingly odd arrangement is justified under various state statutes or institutional administrative guidelines which center on the need to provide all necessary treatment. With the recent expansions of student, prisoner, and patient rights, one can expect that this notion of institutional consent will be further limited in the future.

28

Voluntariness

Once capacity to consent has been established, it is necessary to assure that the consent is voluntary. In terms of legal requirements this usually means the absence of coercion or duress. A basic problem in the behavior change area occurs when a suggestion of reward or punishment accompanies the offer to "voluntarily" enter a treatment program. It may be a direct threat ("Either you go into this program or serve your full term") or an indirect one ("If this program doesn't help you, we'll have to try something more drastic"). Or there may be an offer of reward ("If you enter this program voluntarily we will, of course, inform the parole board"). Consent obtained with the aid of such a "suggestion" lacks the necessary degree of voluntariness.

Perhaps no one in an institutional setting can really volunteer. In *Kaimowitz* an inmate volunteered to undergo psychosurgery in the hopes it would cure him. The state court suggested that an involuntarily confined mental patient could not truly volunteer since the condition of confinement is inherently coercive. The degree to which other courts rely on this as precedent will determine the notion of voluntariness in closed institutions.

Behavior therapists, who work through changing features in the environment in order to change behavior, often argue that "freedom" and "voluntariness" are illusory concepts and that in fact all behavior is coerced to some degree. Some practitioners say that for this reason they do not take the issue of voluntary consent seriously. But they certainly must learn to, if they want to avoid legal challenges in the future.

Informed Consent

If capacity and voluntariness can be established, a client must be informed as to what he is consenting to. If there is a language problem, there can be no "information." So the informing process, both oral and written, should be in the client's native language. The problem of comprehension must be addressed, for many prospective clients may not understand what is being told to them or given to them to read. All information should be at an appropriate comprehension level.

The process should include an opportunity to talk things over with others not involved. The *Wyatt* decision set up Human Rights Committees composed of impartial but knowledgeable individuals. For consent to be truly informed, the client should be able to discuss the procedures with such a panel. The consent forms should indicate the names of others to whom the client talked to assure that such an interchange occurred.

The informing process should also contain a behavioral element.[9] The process is generally a passive one with an individual signing a form or consenting by failing to object. But those in the behavioral sciences can hardly view knowledge as something residing in the mind rather than as a behavior to be exhibited in concrete acts. Thus the process should include some post-test which allows the individual to indicate through positive acts that he understands the significance of the information given him.

The substance about which the client must be informed includes several items. The first item that he must be informed about is his right to refuse to consent. There must not be any conditions or penalties contingent upon this refusal, or else it will destroy the element of voluntariness. He must also be informed of his right to withdraw at any time. There should be no attempt to get him to waive this right, such as telling him that by agreeing to begin this treatment he must continue until it is completed.

Next, the prospective client must be informed of the risks involved in the treatment. These might include short-term and long-term physical and psychological problems and other factors, such as that by entering this program he will have undergone psychological treatment and may have to explain that at a later date when he seeks a job or an insurance policy.

You must also describe the benefits of the approach you propose, specifically the possibility of success in changing some behavior. And you must also discuss the risks and benefits of alternate treatments. One obvious problem with this is that you will have a tendency to stress the benefits of the approach you honestly feel is best and emphasize the risks of other possible approaches. Perhaps to give full meaning to this element of informed consent, some standardized descriptions could be promulgated. The danger in that is that the more established approaches, with more practitioners and more data, would probably fare better, and the more innovative approaches would bear a heavy burden to persuade a client to consent to them.

Some researchers have also raised the objection that such a requirement would destroy research designs, because it might be construed to include control groups. Thus a group which you want to receive no treatment for a while, so that you can compare results from a treatment group, may be presented with an alluring menu of alternative possibilities and leave your control group. The impetus for this last requirement for consent is coming from federal guidelines, and the interaction between seriously concerned researchers and the federal agencies can be expected to produce further changes over the next few months.

Assuming the decision to intervene with a particular individual about a particular behavior is on firm legal ground, the next area for decision is the selection of a strategy.

CHAPTER 3 REVIEW CHECKLIST

1. Do you have consent to be in contact with the prospective client to gain information that may justify an intervention?

2. Are your institution's procedures for consent specific and written down?

3. Is the consent process conducted in the native language of the prospective client and at his level of verbal comprehension?

4. Are the procedures read to him as well as given in

written form?

5. Does the prospective client have the capacity to consent?

6. If the client lacks capacity and you must obtain consent elsewhere, do you still explain the entire process to the client?

7. Was consent free of any implied promises or threats which might constitute duress or coercion?

8. Is the client fully informed of what the procedure entails, along with any risks and benefits, as well as being informed about alternative procedures?

9. Has the client had an opportunity to talk about the process with any impartial outsiders?

10. Does the client know he may refuse to consent, and that even after consenting he may revoke his consent at any time?

11. Does the client consent to the release, publication or other use of data contemplated during the project or after the client leaves the project?

12. Do you have a signed form which deals with each of the above?

13. Did the consent process contain an element in which the client was asked to exhibit behavior, apart from simply signing a form, indicating he understands?

4

Selecting a Strategy

SUMMARY

Selection of a strategy involves questions of both procedure and substance. Procedural decisions include whether to focus on the individual or change someone in his environment, whether to treat individually or in a group, whether to attempt an experiment or restrict yourself to conventional modes of treatment, whether to treat in the present environment or remove the client to another, and whether your procedure faces durational constraints.

The law does not prefer the substance of one strategy over another, but one should be familiar with advantages and disadvantages of a range of alternatives: psychosurgery, electrical stimulation of the brain, shock treatment, genetic manipulation, various drug therapies, traditional psychotherapy, group pressure, and structured learning. This chapter describes the legal consequences of various procedural alternatives and shows how the legal tests of restrictiveness and effectiveness are applied to commonly used strategies.

PROCEDURAL DECISIONS

Changing Individuals or Environments?

An initial decision in selecting a general procedure is whether to concentrate on the proposed client or on someone else in his environment. Every counselor who works with families sees a child who is not really the problem, and the counselor may feel the solution to the real problem is to change the parents. Prison counselors see inmates with no history of violence who are accused of assaulting a guard or fellow inmate. School counselors who see children referred for corrective action may realize that one particular teacher is involved in a disproportionate number of cases. A mental health professional evaluating patients may see that one staff member's patients seem to get worse rather than better.

So do you attack the crisis behavior being complained about and leave it at that, or do you focus on someone else in the environment? An initial legal problem is that you probably have authority to treat the client but no authority over parents, teachers, guards, peers, and others. But you also know that correcting some behavior in a vacuum and then returning the individual to the unchanged environment will so predictably be ineffective that it may fall below legal standards.

So you must try to change the environment. A first step is directly aimed at a problem staff member. Perhaps you have the authority to hire, retrain, or otherwise influence staff along the lines detailed in Chapter 9. If not, then perhaps you can gather present staff in a group at the next in-service session and try to direct change in that way. A supervisor may say, "You were hired to work with the clients, not the staff," or an employee union may object to having a staff person be the subject of an unsolicited psychological intervention. If so, you may have to try a less direct approach.

One approach is to teach the client as much as possible about how his behavior influences, and is influenced by, the others in his environment. In a novel school project in California,[1] a consultant was asked to change the behavior of several children who were deemed intolerable. He taught them how to be polite to their teachers, to ask respectfully for explanations of material they did not understand, and to be demonstrably enthusiastic when they did understand. Within a few weeks the teachers stopped complaining about the children and found them responsive and eager to learn. Work with the students had thus changed the behavior of their teachers.

So your strategy may be to help the client himself change someone in his environment. If that is not successful and you still feel the client is not the real problem, your only alternative is to resist efforts to force behavior change. Otherwise you will be entering into a program that may face a legal challenge before it is completed.

Individual or Group Treatments?

The next decision should be whether to treat the client individually or in a group. There is no inherent legal right to one type of treatment or the other so long as there are individual treatment plans.[2] However, some forms of group treatment really amount to attempts to evade treatment responsibility.[3] It is true that, since environments shape behavior, exposure to any group will cause change, but that change might not meet legal requirements. The normal interactions between a mental patient and other patients and staff cannot be viewed as treatment even when dignified with a label such as "milieu therapy."[4] There is a definite legal right to an individual treatment program.

Another danger in group environments is that behavior might worsen, and the client has a definite right not to be made worse. It is common to hear juvenile facilities referred to as "schools for crime," obviously admitting that behavior is worsened through treatment. Therapists having to do social effectiveness training with mental patients being returned to the community face the fact that inmates have lost needed social skills.[5] In school, if an occasionally disruptive student is transferred to a whole class of disruptive students, no one should be surprised if he learns some new tricks. Some parents complain that their retarded children, after years in an institution, are able to do less than before they were admitted. Exposure to a homogeneous group where the client will tend toward dysfunctional behavior (acquiring bad skills or losing good ones) may not only be poor therapy, but may violate a client's right not to be made worse.

There is a similar right—more vigorously enforced—not to be physically abused. If your selection of strategy creates a group that cannot possibly be kept under control, so that there are fights or sexual assaults, then such a group is not

35

legally tolerable.[6]

This does not mean you cannot employ a group strategy. School personnel must often work with groups. The economics and logistics of counseling may dictate group work. And in fact there seem to be some prohibitions against separating clients out for individual treatment. Current educational trends as well as legal requirements[7] suggest that students who were at one time kept at home because of some handicap must now be "mainstreamed" into the regular school operation. This comes partly as a realization that since environments teach social skills, a young handicapped person should learn in a normal environment, not in a group of similarly handicapped persons or alone.

Your strategy will depend on the client's need, but unless there is a compelling reason to isolate the person then he will likely be in some group. That is permissible so long as there is an individual treatment plan and the client gets better, not worse.

Experimental Versus Accepted Approaches

The next determination is whether the strategy will be accepted treatment or experimental.[8] It is hard to define the legally important distinctions between the two. Accepted treatment would encompass a broad range of approaches that might be followed by a majority of reasonable practitioners. The goal would certainly be to "cure" the problem. An experiment would be less tried and tested; research documentation would be part of the goal of the program; and "seeing what happens" for a class of people would be as important as solving the problem finally for any one client in particular.

What is accepted practice within the profession will not necessarily be judged as such by the lay public or in the courts. In one county school district I have visited, there are two schools with a substantial number of students in a token economy system (earning points to trade for rewards). In one project, the counselor in charge had read of similar systems for several years in a wide array of publications. He had seen some in operation. He was not involved in research but was faced with a real need to reach a large group of severely underachieving and often disruptive students. He set up a program which, as in any good behavioral effort, had sufficient data feeding back to indicate if it was doing any good. If it had not worked, he would have abandoned it and tried something else rather than continuing just to see what would happen. As the program developed, he thought up a few things he had never read of in the literature and tried them out. The program has now completed its second year. Is this an experiment? Everyone concerned with it considers it an imaginative and ambitious program, but not out of the range of the flexible methods needed to deal with the ever-changing problems facing schools.

But a few miles away is a very similar project which proclaims itself an experiment. It receives federal funds which would not be available if it did not call itself experimental. As an experiment it has followed elaborate procedures to gain parental consent, and it has been gathering a lot of data. It would probably continue for the life of the grant whether it was producing results or not.

The question of whether your strategy is *intended* to be experimental or an accepted mode of practice is probably important only if someone complains and tries to have it stopped. In that case, an experiment must have many more safeguards such as obtaining consent, there must be a clear explanation of the risks and possible benefits, and there must be some public good to be gained from engaging in the experiment. There is a risk:benefit ratio involved in accepted practice also—no approach is guaranteed to bring a benefit, and any approach can go wrong and entail some risk, but it can be demonstrated through professional literature and widespread practice that the benefit consistently outweighs a risk which is negligible. In an experiment, there has not been enough testing to assure that the risk is negligible or that the benefit will outweigh it.

In another example, a Florida school operated under a Department of Defense contract sought to alter troublesome behavior by injections of urine into the blood.[9] Among other treatment techniques used, school personnel also shackled offenders, used electric dog training collars, and forced children to spend the night in graves they had dug themselves. The program's administrators did not consider these procedures experimental, but a Congressional investigating committee felt no benefit had ever been demonstrated for any of these methods and the risk to psychological well-being seemed incalculably large. So even if it is not intended to be an experiment, a body inquiring into your program might decide otherwise and apply stricter standards to your work than you have been observing.

Even if your method has been thoroughly tested and widely used, if you employ it for a new purpose it might be experimental. When electroconvulsive therapy is used, the drug anectine is administered to prevent physical harm during convulsions. In electroconvulsive therapy its effect of respiratory paralysis is immediately counteracted so that its only effect is relaxation. A few behavior change experimenters in California prisons began using the drug by itself, in order to produce this very aversive feeling of suffocation, so that the prisoner would avoid the behavior that had led to this treatment. They claimed it was not experimental because the drug had been so widely used for so many years, but they were forced to stop.[10]

So as you select a strategy, determine if you are using something so novel, or applying it in such a novel way, that you are in effect conducting an experiment. If so, your clients should be volunteers, you must be able to clearly detail risks and benefits, the benefit:risk ratio must be substantial, there must be a general public interest in undertaking the experiment, the information should not be obtainable in any other way, and the results must be carefully gathered through a well-planned research design. If you are not prepared to meet each of these criteria then you must leave experimental techniques to others.

This does not mean you cannot deviate from traditional practice, attempt to find something better, and even conduct research on your effort, so long as you assure there is not a large risk involved. In a school with several classes of under-achieving students, some might be kept on a traditional approach while others are put in a group token economy system and others in an individualized contingency contract-ing system (contracting to receive certain rewards contingent upon successful completion of specified tasks). Then at appropriate periods you might compare data from a variety of sources and let your research data indicate which approach seems to serve student needs best. The state has a compelling interest to incorporate new approaches; this interest is not served by slavishly adhering to the status quo.

Present Environment or a New One?

The next decision in selection of a strategy is whether you should deal with the client in his present environment or transfer him to a new one. The former alternative poses far fewer legal problems, unless the present environment holds a threat of harm to the client or to others. There is also great logic in it. To remove a person from the environment where certain behavior occurred and place him elsewhere may so change the behavior that you will have little to work on, and upon returning him to the original environment the problem behavior is likely to begin again.

But the practical problem is that you may be told to remove the person from his present environment. He may be a disruptive student or prisoner, or he may be tearing up a family. To suggest that he is better left in the home or class-room is to meet with an expected outcry (and perhaps the suggestion that you should start earning your money).

If you have no choice and must transfer the individual to another setting, then you should follow the due process requirements detailed in Chapter 1. But if you have a choice, far fewer problems and far better treatment are likely to occur if you can keep the client in the same environment.

If the transfer means placement in an institution, you must first exhaust all other less restrictive alternatives and show that they will not be adequate. You must provide that the client's right against being harmed or having behavior deteriorate will be protected. You have an almost impossible task to show that your client will benefit from institutionalization at all, let alone that it will be more beneficial than treatment in the current environment. The only likely exception is where failing to confine the client presents a clearly demonstrated danger to others.

Finally, if you do recommend a strategy involving institutionalization you must provide for periodic reviews of progress with release built into the program. If you oversee institutionalization with no progress and no release, you may be liable for damages. Institutionalization is literally the last resort for both legal and therapeutic reasons.

Durational Limits

The next area of difficulty in selecting a strategy is defining the length of time required to produce results. The initial response is usually "I'll certainly try for change as quickly as possible and work on it for as long as necessary." In addition, the conditions on your relationship to the client may dictate durational constraints: A school child may have only the rest of the school term, a patient may have ninety days until release, a prisoner may have a time limit on his sentence. So you must select a strategy which can reasonably bring change in the time you have.

If there is not an actual time constraint, do you face some durational limitation gauged by effectiveness? For example, if you are attempting some psychoanalytic insight therapy which goes on for months with no demonstrable results, will your program be terminated? Courts are beginning to require periodic reviews of progress of involuntarily confined patients and might order release if progress is not found. A speaker at the 1974 Isaac Ray Symposium [11] who prefers the opportunity for long-term psychiatric treatment commented that if faced with an arbitrary durational limit—for example, cause a change in six months or stop—he would have to use behavior modification methods, which he clearly did not like. If the judicial suggestions of durational limits grow stronger, subjective counselor preferences may give way to objective evidence of client progress.

A final durational consideration may influence the severity of your strategy. If an aversive treatment over a brief period will remediate symptoms, then is it truly more "aversive" than a milder treatment which takes years? The legal trend is to require the least restrictive alternative. Is a lengthy confinement in an easy-going therapy less restrictive or more restrictive than an aversive or even coerced therapy pursued for only a few weeks? No court has yet faced this question, but you may have to.

We have so far considered several procedural problems: whether to treat the environment or the individual; whether to concentrate on the individual or to treat in a group; whether to attempt an experiment or restrict yourself to accepted modes of treatment; whether to treat in the current environment or remove the client to another; and whether your strategy faces durational constraints. Now we should proceed to a different type of concern—the substance of the strategy.

ALTERNATIVE STRATEGIES

In selecting a strategy for behavior change, the practitioner is faced with a wide range of alternatives. There are some treatments which are controversial and receive a lot of publicity. The law does not, as yet, prefer one type of strategy over another. However your strategy should be as good as alternatives. You should know about other possible approaches both to choose your strategy and to counsel clients about strategies to avoid; review all alternatives and rate them from most desirable to least desirable with respect to the particular problem. The main legal test to be applied to any strategy is whether a balance between effectiveness and restrictiveness is established.

In examining these alternatives we can start with the most controversial and legally contestable approaches.

Psychosurgery

Psychosurgery is advocated by some to alter behavior. A dose of anaesthetic followed by destruction of brain cells will probably alter behavior but not predictably for better or for worse and not specifically in regard to a discrete complained-of behavior.[12]

The reason such a bizarre technique must be taken seriously is that it is actually proposed as a solution to common problems. Some psychosurgeons claim a "cure" for hyperactivity, so even a school psychologist facing parents with a hyperactive child and trying to enlist their support in a behavior change program might face a bias toward a seemingly quick and total cure like psychosurgery.

Brain surgery is a highly developed skill, practiced with great care and effecting often miraculous results in dealing with physical symptoms. But psychosurgery—surgery to alter some psychological trait—is experimental, unproven, and irreversible in its effects. It may seem effective in masking a behavior; for example, an aggressive prisoner who is dulled by surgery will probably not exhibit aggressive behavior. But surgery cannot create an affirmative behavior, as would occur in a therapy where the aggressive person learns to control himself and thus displays a new skill. The existing record shows that psychosurgery not only does not produce proven benefits but also has a very high risk.[13]

When critics of behavior modification speak, they are often referring to psychosurgery experiments with involuntary patients, and one might wish this whole controversial area would be discontinued. But physicians have continued to receive research grants, and research in this area will continue in the future.

Electrical Stimulation of the Brain

Electrical stimulation of the brain is getting more publicity. Most research is on animals as yet, but results are dramatic. One theory is that different parts of the brain control different behaviors and that by implanting tiny wires to electrically activate those parts, the animal's behavior can be dictated. The practical applications of this approach are quite remote, except that a pleasure center and a pain center can be easily activated. Thus if someone monitors a subject's behavior and the subject is doing what is desired a pleasurable sensation can immediately be imparted. And conversely, if an undesired behavior is engaged in, sufficient pain can be imparted to cause a halt.[14]

The behavioral paradigm suggests that the learning experience be structured so that the pleasure of success follows accomplishment. Where an undesired behavior is the target, one tries to allow natural punishers to discourage repetition. The danger is that some behavioral scientists will no doubt be intrigued by the dramatic effects they can get in a short time through electrical stimulation of the brain. You would not have to worry about structuring an environment to teach a new behavior, selecting appropriate reinforcers and punishers, determining how to administer them, and so forth; you would simply wire into the brain and instantly reward behavior you wanted and punish behavior you did not want.

Once the researcher has hooked into the brain it will be hard to convince him to let go, and proposed research projects indicate how far some practitioners would take this approach. Currently it can be administered only when the subject is being observed. But some researchers would like to use the brain hookup and other electrophysiological instrumentation to monitor and control behavior when the client is out of sight.[15]

Some researchers theorize that electrical activity of the brain precedes violent episodes, and that monitoring of this activity would allow a computer to send out a signal that would either neutralize the activity or, more likely, incapacitate the individual. There is therefore no way of telling whether it works—that is, whether the person might have actually become violent—because he would never have the chance. The subject would merely double up every once in a while. And we would hope it would not happen while he is driving a car on a freeway.

Other electrophysiological researchers would monitor

physical symptoms such as respiration, pulse, blood pressure, and adrenalin. They theorize that certain physical patterns exist in certain behaviors such as sexual excitation. If the subject is a sex offender, for example, and the computer monitor discovered the indicators of excitation it could send out an incapacitating signal.

One more ambitious proposal [16] would monitor the physical location of an individual such as a parolee, and when the computer showed the individual had crossed into a prohibited zone, he would be zapped until he returned to the prescribed area. The argument advanced in favor of these schemes is that they would "free" persons from prisons and mental institutions because they could be safely monitored and supervised on the street. That is a rather illusory idea of freedom. These researchers admit the obvious fact that the client would unplug himself from the computer's grasp as soon as he left the sight of the behavioral scientist. The predictable response has been to develop instruments which cannot be removed.

From a constitutional perspective, many questions are raised. This is not the proper place to detail the many possible objections [17] but realize that the law works on precedents. Once one barrier is broken, such as forcing a subject to wear a monitoring device, then another may follow, such as constantly searching and seizing his body for information, and then another, such as executing punishment summarily, without due process. Once each step is allowed, it makes it easier for the next step. So one might argue that none of this should be tolerated, that in fact all such research should be prohibited.

The problem is that some of the techniques hold great promise for voluntary treatment in important areas. The electronic pacemaker worn by some individuals to monitor heart rhythm and send a signal to correct irregularity is a good example. Suppose an epileptic could wear a small device that could monitor brain activity and send an electric signal (not painful) to neutralize seizures? So we cannot simply order a halt to such research.

We cannot proscribe the range of treatment either. Alcoholics, homosexuals, and transvestites have reportedly been treated voluntarily by carrying electrical instruments and, upon perceiving themselves about to engage in a behavior that they no longer want to display, administering a shock to themselves.[18]

So the crucial factor seems to be voluntariness and private treatment. The law does not currently allow such electrophysiological monitoring and brain stimulating instrumentation to be used coercively or in state-run programs by agents of the state. Those interested in responsible behavior change programs must question whether it should ever be allowed.

Shock Treatment

Another type of medically oriented strategy to change behavior by affecting the brain is electroconvulsive therapy, often referred to as shock therapy. There is no real agreement on whether this works from a medical perspective.[19] Why would throwing a person into convulsions have any effect on his behavior? Some have theorized that epileptics are not schizophrenic, and that inducing an epileptic-like seizure in a schizophrenic would reintegrate a split personality. That theory is as clear as the label "schizophrenic." Others have suggested that the experience of the shock treatment weakens the mind's ability to hold on to the layers of defenses it has been building up, and that as they slip away normalcy is able to reassert itself.

From another perspective one might suggest that the therapy is very punishing and that if it follows some definite behavior the subject is likely to drop that behavior, or at least avoid detection in the future. In fact, in one widely cited example a behavior modifier exhorted his clients in a Vietnamese hospital, "Anyone too sick to work ("work" involved physical danger) begins treatment tomorrow." The treatment was electroconvulsive therapy and the message was clear—it was intended as punishment.[20]

There is little evidence to suggest that shock treatment

works better than any other therapy, or better than no therapy at all, but some very frustrated clients want immediate cures, and there are some physicians who will recommend it. ✷

Genetic Manipulation

The strategies mentioned above—psychosurgery, electrical stimulation of the brain, and electroconvulsive therapy—are proposed by those who feel the key to all deviant behavior is in the brain. Another group of scientists argue that the key is in the genes and that the strategy must be to manipulate the genetic structure.[21]

They propose to prohibit marriages between persons carrying certain genetic endowments on the grounds that their offspring will be likely to exhibit undesirable behavior. The law does not tolerate such preventive techniques. These researchers then argue that if such persons marry, they should be sterilized. The law has unfortunately allowed this in certain narrow cases but only after children with behavior problems had already been born, not upon a prediction based on some genetic configuration.[22]

Geneticists also argue that even if such persons marry and give birth, the genetic structure can be manipulated to prevent future aberrant behavior. Other geneticists point out that such genetic tampering could also alter the body's immunity mechanisms, with the result that the baby would be likely to die before it got around to exhibiting much of any behavior, acceptable or unacceptable.[23]

Researchers persist with attempts to link aggression to an extra chromosome and so forth. The significance of all this effort is that it suggests that a person's behavior is determined by his parents at his conception, that the genetic makeup can be examined in some screening process before birth or afterward, and that the strategy for behavior change should be genetic manipulation. That leaves little for a school psychologist or other behavioral counselor to do, and in fact the success that such behavioral counselors have had in altering behavior certainly counters the geneticists' argument.

46

Another strategy for changing behavior by intruding into the body involves dealing with body chemistry. There seem to be six main strategies: psychopharmacology; suggestibility; suppression; relaxation; nausea; and paralysis.

Psychopharmacology. Psychopharmacology involves an attempt to alter the brain's chemical structure in order to alter the individual's behavior. This area of study is certainly in an infant state, and no particular chemical has been shown to cause a particular behavior. One branch of this is getting many headlines, however, and possibly will yield some concrete results. Researchers dealing with nutrition have suggested that certain chemical food additives, particularly those found in "junk foods" that children love, can cause a hyperactive pattern of behavior.[24] Removal of such chemicals, they claim, will terminate the behavior. This is a highly fruitful area of inquiry because the alarming incidence of so-called hyperactivity bears a general correlation to the incidence of unnatural chemicals added to our food. It would certainly be a waste to bring an elaborate program into play as a strategy for dealing with an individual's behavior if a change in diet could do the same thing; it would also be tragic to use such foods as rewards in a behavior modification program.

Some researchers in nutrition have concentrated on the role of vitamins.[25] The absence of certain vitamins may correlate with certain behaviors, particularly sudden fits of anger or depression. Unfortunately, the introduction of vitamins back into the body in the form of chemical substances does not seem to guarantee a change. Other researchers concentrate on blood-sugar level and its effect on the work of the brain.[26] Since hypoglycemia (low blood sugar) is a recognized disease, the research has concentrated more on physical symptoms than on behavior. But when swings in sugar level are controlled, a more stable mental state also seems to be present. The research continues, and its results will likely be an important adjunct to other strategies.

The important feature from a legal view is that while as yet unproven therapies should not be relied on, the practitioner should not engage in unnecessary treatment. So you should not confine a youth for a year in a rigorous program if dietary manipulation over a period of weeks might be as effective.

Suggestibility. Another chemical strategy has to do with suggestibility, which is almost like hypnosis. Certain drugs apparently place an individual in a trance-like state in which their ability to resist therapist's suggestions is greatly lowered. The therapist's suggestions are usually about behavior not to be engaged in again.[27] If the drugging experience is aversive to the client, that factor may suppress the behavior just as much as the post-drugging suggestions. In any event, the evidence is unclear whether it works for even a short time. Because of its similarity to "brainwashing" it is certainly not a strategy which the law looks upon with favor.

Suppression. The third general effect of drugs—to suppress behavior—is quite commonly used with school children diagnosed as discipline problems. There are indications of widespread abuse of such drugs and of schools pressuring parents into giving them to children.[28] A Congressional investigation[29] revealed that some drug companies had salesmen appear at PTA meetings to convince teachers and parents of the better life through chemistry.

One obvious impetus to using drugs on children is to get quick and easy results: A counselor does not have to work very hard while all his clients are drugged. Another is the belief that a child will "grow out of" the problem behavior, whether it is hyperactivity in school or bed-wetting at home. The theory is that, if you can only mask the symptoms with drugs, one day the problem will be gone. Extensive research has found the opposite.[30] Some of the drugs are highly dangerous to children, causing death or physiological addiction. It seems logical that being told for years to take a pill to cure your behavior problem can lead to a psychological dependence that will generalize to other drugs in the adolescent years. And, ironically, once the drugs are discontinued the behavior is likely to recur.

Drugging to suppress behavior is common in mental

health cases. Medical journals are filled with ads proclaiming the virtue of drugs to aid in "managing" your patient. Real legal questions arise: whether suppression is treatment; whether it is as effective as other therapies; and whether it is less restrictive. Remember the earlier questions—whether the individual needs to be treated and whether you have a right to treat the particular behavior complained of. If so, then is suppressing the symptoms—masking them with drugs—an acceptable form of treatment?

Treatment is usually an intervention that lasts some period of time and is then terminated: This would be thought of as a cure. If a physician said, "We have no cure for your problem, but we'll suppress the symptoms for the rest of your life," would that be acceptable? In some cases, such as chemotherapy for cancer, it might be. Many patients willingly take medication for extensive periods. But what of a strategy for behavior change? Would not permanent medication be so much more restrictive than a shorter, different type of therapy? And what of the side effects of drugs? Instead of dealing with one pinpointed behavior and treating it, drugs might mask or alter a wider range of behaviors. Isn't that "restrictive"?

And what of effectiveness? If a behavior is merely suppressed, rather than alternative positive behaviors being learned, and if the drugs must be continued indefinitely, doesn't that suggest that this type of therapy is less than effective? These points have not yet been decided finally by the courts but, consistent with other judicial decisions, drugging for permanent suppression of behavior is a less desirable strategy than others we will discuss.[31]

Relaxation. Drugs are also used to relax an individual so that other strategies can work. Where an individual is so keyed up, overwrought, or even physically tense that a counselor cannot even communicate, or the client literally cannot get his physical behavior under control, drugs might be used to calm him. The test of effectiveness and restrictiveness of such use of drugs should be whether it is aimed at *physiological* symptoms rather than the actual behavior complained of, whether it can be phased out after a short time, and whether it is used merely to relax the client rather than to increase suggestibility.

Aversive consequences: Nausea. Chemicals are also used to change behavior by causing nausea. One drug has been paired with alcohol in an attempt to condition a subject so that a drink does not bring pleasure but rather brings an hour of uncontrollable vomiting.[32] Research suggests this is remarkably ineffective and conditions the client to avoid the treatment, not to avoid alcohol.

Nausea-producing drugs are also used to condition other behavior such as homosexuality. A typical treatment would structure a homosexually arousing experience so that it would be followed by the drug and the accompanying intense nausea.[33] If the strategy worked, then it might make sense, assuming that drinking and sexual conduct are areas that are within your rights to attempt to alter. But research does not suggest very consistent results.

Punishment: Paralysis. A final use of drugs is as punishment. In addition to nausea, some drugs can cause a muscular paralysis which includes the respiratory system so that the subject cannot breathe and begins to suffocate. Persons subjected to this have confirmed that it is terrifying. One cannot imagine a client volunteering to be administered such a drug. The chief psychiatrist at California's Vacaville prison, who uses this approach, has stated, "Even the toughest inmates have come to fear and hate the drug. I don't blame them. I wouldn't have one treatment myself for the world."[34]

This strategy to alter behavior through punishment carries the legal burdens of any coerced therapy. In addition, since it is clearly intended as punishment it may fall within constitutional prohibitions against cruel and unusual punishment. If it is aversive therapy administered once to stop a really gross behavior then it might be tolerated. But if the offense is slight, such as swearing or smoking where prohibited,[35] then the punishment is plainly "cruel." (Unfortunately, in some prisons it is not so "unusual.") But most damning from a legal and therapeutic sense is that it is not effective in changing behavior.

The remaining strategies are the ones most likely to be encountered in public programs. They are your best choices although they are not without legal problems. It is hard to separate and catalog techniques because any one program might use several overlapping approaches. But generally we can suggest three groupings: traditional psychotherapeutic sessions, intense group pressure situations, and structured learning.

Traditional Psychotherapy

Traditional psychotherapy includes talking to a client, finding out what seems to be the problem, and helping to find a solution. The theory is that the talking will help the client gain insight, and once having gained insight, the client can take it from there.

This therapy is quite limited if the client does not see himself as having any problem, or if the client cannot readily verbalize about himself (often a problem in schools with younger children, prisons with hostile or semi-literate prisoners, and mental institutions with clients who simply will not talk), or if the client and counselor cannot agree on the problem. One correctional counselor at a facility near Washington, D.C. told about a very hostile youth who, when asked what was bothering him, said, "I'm locked up behind bars." The counselor replied, "No, that's not it. Come on, what's really bothering you?" The counselor explained, somewhat puzzled, that he never did get anywhere with the youth.

It is often more helpful to get a person talking and thinking about the "problem" by placing him with others similarly situated. Such group sessions are called by various names: encounter, awareness, communication training, sensitivity training, and so forth. The theory is that a person will gain insight into his problems and be able to communicate them better after hearing and seeing others grapple with similar difficulties. Formats vary from just getting together for awhile to elaborate role-playing and other exercises.

But the key ingredient always remains verbal insight. Research does not indicate that such insight necessarily changes behavior. It further indicates that whatever may be learned in the context of one group may not necessarily transfer to another context.[36]

From a legal standpoint this type of therapy is certainly not regarded as restrictive. However there are two main problems. First, it may cause harm. Groups, improperly supervised, can destroy vulnerable members. Second, it may not amount to much in the way of treatment. "Insight" is an illusory goal, and it is hard for anyone but the therapist to tell if it is being reached. If release, or assignment to some other program, is dependent upon some goal being achieved in a psychotherapeutic setting then release might either be premature or it may be indefinitely delayed. Some inmates have observed that once they begin using the right catchphrases—"I am gaining insight into my problem," "I am getting in touch with my feelings," or "I am beginning to accept responsibility for my behavior"—they are likely to gain a discharge from the therapy if not from the institution itself. Thus using a nondirective approach with no concrete method of ascertaining progress can lead to release before behavior has actually been changed. Conversely, if the client has not reached this vague goal after several years, which is not unusual, there may be vulnerability to a charge that no treatment is occurring.

Group Pressure

A second type of strategy involves group management but in a more directed manner. The basic idea is intense peer pressure to force a conforming behavior change. A new member to the group may be torn down when he resists the group and then reinforced when he conforms. This is, of course, the traditional military model. It is also used by many community-based anti-drug or anti-alcohol treatment programs. There is little research to support the "basic training" model, and some research suggests it is less effective than more humane approaches.[37]

One large problem with this approach is that the group can develop a dynamic of its own and may change a client in a direction that is not necessarily rehabilitative. If it makes him worse, the supervisor may be in real trouble.

A very controversial federally funded group program with youthful drug offenders in Dade County, Florida was called "The Seed" (and its participants were called seedlings). A study [38] by the Comprehensive Health Planning Council of South Florida described the program. For the first few days, the new seedling is prohibited from speaking. Then he is forced into continuous group confrontation aimed at extracting a confession. "This process breaks down a person's dependence on his psychological defenses and creates a dependency upon the support of the group. The group responds to the person's admission and confession of failures and personal disabilities with supportive statements of love and respect. . . . The peer group then becomes both the conscience and the support mechanism for changed behavior." Several counselors analyzing the effect of the program noted that seedlings could no longer cope on their own but instead slavishly followed their peers. Can anyone call that rehabilitation? [39]

Some school systems are now proposing special schools where the students would be pressured into displaying nationalism, unquestioning obedience, and other "virtues." [40] Another name for this behavior change strategy is indoctrination, and it is sufficiently foreign to our concept of education that it can be expected to provoke legal challenges.

Structured Learning

Structured social learning is based on the proposition that learning behavior in a social context seems to follow some basic rules: Those things which we succeed at and receive social approval for, we tend to do more often; those things which we fail at or are punished for, we tend to avoid. [41] We initiate most behaviors in imitation of others and then shape them over time in small increments depending upon what is reinforced, what is ignored, and what brings an unpleasant response from others. What we learn in one social context does not necessarily generalize to another context—thus children may be completely different people in school and at home, and rehabilitated mental patients who do well in the institution may act differently back in their old environment.

Observing these phenomena, practitioners of structured social learning establish goal behaviors, break those terminal behaviors down into small sequential steps, model each step so the client can see what is expected, rehearse the behaviors in a non-threatening social context, reinforce successful performance until the behavior stands on its own, and then, once the terminal behavior is reached, arrange contingencies in the natural environment so that the desired level of the new behavior will be maintained.

This is an "ideal" model which is difficult to achieve in practice. If no specific goal is formulated, then the rest of the program falls. If the tasks (small steps leading to the goal) are too large or are improperly sequenced, then the experience may be a punishing failure. If a step needs to be modeled to give the client the idea, but is not, the client may never progress. If initial attempts at performance are ignored or punished (as in a group which picks apart a client's attempt at a new level of skill), then the client may regress. The most common source of failure occurs when a successful level is attained in a structured environment but is not reinforced enough to maintain it in the natural environment. Thus the intervention was "successful" as long as it lasted, but the effects soon disappear.

In addition to the problem of effectiveness, several other legal problems typically arise: Is the structured environment too restrictive; is the goal a suitable one; are the tasks odious to perform (perhaps amounting to unauthorized punishment); is the reinforcement structure aversive; will a continuation of the program into the natural environment represent an invasion of privacy? Later chapters will deal with these problems of goals, tasks, and motivation.

CHAPTER 4 REVIEW CHECKLIST

1. Could you solve the problem by changing someone else's behavior?

2. Will changing the client's behavior be ineffective unless you also change someone else's behavior?

3. Can you teach the client to change that other person's behavior?

4. Do you have an individual treatment plan?

5. Are you making sure the individual, particularly if he's in a group, is not worsening?

6. Does your individual treatment needlessly isolate the client from others?

7. Should your approach be considered experimental and, if so, do you take extra precautions?

8. If your approach causes a person to be transferred to a new environment, did you consider less restrictive alternatives first, and did you follow due process requirements?

9. Do you review progress at reasonably short intervals, with a change in strategy or release from the program if no progress can be found?

10. If psychosurgery, electrical stimulation of the brain, or electroconvulsive therapy is associated with your approach or your institution, can you prove that less drastic alternatives do not work?

11. If you use drugs, are you merely masking symptoms or are you working toward a positive change in some behavior?

12. If you use drugs for aversive conditioning or punishment, can you show that less drastic means failed, your approach produces positive results, and you are not violating prohibitions against cruel, unusual punishment?

13. If you use psychotherapy, can you show positive progress after a period of, for example, six months, in case a court inquires?

14. If you use peer pressure, can you show you are changing behavior in a way that will be maintained after the client leaves the group?

15. If you use structured learning, is the structure sufficiently different from traditional rewards and punishments to qualify as treatment?

5

Establishing Goals

SUMMARY

The goal of a behavior change project should be related to the behavior which justified the intervention of the state in the first place. The goal should thus be to change that behavior so that the state involvement can be terminated. The change should basically benefit the individual and should not look for its justification too far outward into society's needs or too far inward into institutional convenience. An individual's behavior should not be the focus of change when changing something else in the environment can solve the problem. It should never be your goal to change behavior which is constitutionally protected. Chapter 5 describes the range of program goals that would be compatible with legal requirements and that would provide sufficient focus for an adequate program of behavior change.

PRIORITIES IN ESTABLISHING GOALS

The only acceptable goal for any public program of behavior change should be to change overt behavior. It should not be a goal to change a person's mind or his attitude.[1] The reason, from a behavioral science viewpoint, is simple: Technique and success in dealing with observable behavior can be evaluated, but there are few safeguards when the purpose is to change something which only the treating practitioner can determine is getting better or worse. One might certainly delve into subjective matters such as how a client feels about something, but the program goal should be established in observable terms.

The choice of an observable target behavior involves a balancing of interests between the individual's need for change and society's desire for change. So an initial question must always be asked—for whose benefit is this behavior change being undertaken—and the answer should be found in the goal.

What is Society's Interest?

Society's *specific* interest is served by laws and regulations prohibiting certain conduct and providing either expressly or by implication for behavior change to prevent it from occurring again. In cases where no specific behavior has occurred, but where there are concerns about the "danger" that an individual poses to himself or to others, a social interest is served by carrying out some treatment, or if that is not effective, confining the person. This kind of predictive judgment is very hard to make, and the case can be made that the danger to society of locking up individuals who have committed no offending behavior is greater than the danger to society of allowing persons to remain free who may be harmful only at some point in the future.[2]

Society's *general* interest is protected by a notion of normal behavior, or a range of behavior that will be tolerated. Outside that range, the behavior is "deviant" and the individual will presumably be subjected to great pressure to return to the norm. But society also has a general interest in diversity, in tolerating differences and respecting and nurturing the right to be different.

In some behavior change projects there is a tendency to promote a general conformity. All children, for example, might be pressured to say "Yes, sir" or "Yes, ma'am" to adults. In one school project, any child adopting "inappropriate" sex role behaviors is immediately the subject of a program of change. In some prisons, swearing is often the subject of reprisals or even treatment. In projects in prisons, mental institutions, and residential schools, clients are often required to make their beds and clean their rooms.

All of these programs are in the name of normal—someone's idea of what everybody should be like. They raise several questions. Who decides what is normal or desired or appropriate behavior? For whose benefit is behavior changed: Does the institution have a right to change behavior just to make things run more smoothly; do researchers have the right to change behavior for the purposes of research? And most importantly, is the goal properly related to the purpose for which the state has become involved in the first place?

Who Decides What is Normal?

In speaking of society, and society's rights and needs, we are really talking about the balancing of various diverse interests. Those who desire civil liberty for individuals through restraint upon government agents are as much a part of society as those who advocate stopping deviant behavior by allowing the government more latitude in dealing with dissidents.

But society is poorly represented inside our public institutions. In prisons and mental hospitals we find mainly the poor and minority groups. So behavior change programs, as they take place in public institutions, are generally conducted upon society's "losers." In schools, which should represent all of society, the area schools selected for projects are often the worst ones, but unfortunately this means that poor and black kids are likely to be the subjects. Even where the program can draw from a wider base there is some evidence that middle-class white students are dealt with differently, and that poorer black students are the ones assigned to special programs.[3]

This amplifies the importance of the question what is normal and who makes that decision. If an institution catering to white middle-class values and operated by white middle-class citizens deals with poor blacks, then the establishment of goals will always be suspect. Worse, the types of behavior toward which the subject will be pushed in the program may bear no relationship to successful or even normative behavior in the culture to which the individual will return. The program's focus may be not on the type of behavior that got the person into the program in the first place, but on the many small behaviors that seem to clash with majority culture norms (swearing, not saying "Yes, sir," lateness to appointments, lack of goals, physical aggressiveness, sexual promiscuity, poor hygiene, and so forth). Administrators must constantly ask themselves what right they have to even be interested in such things, let alone attempt to change them, unless they bear a direct relationship to the problem behavior which initiated the intervention, or to the achievement of the goal which will terminate the intervention.

One solution would be to have a direct representation of societal interests in reviewing goals, preferably including local community or even "subculture" representation. In *Donaldson* the court noted that the reason for treatment was "to restore the capacity for independent community living." It follows, therefore, that some representative of the community in which the prisoner, disruptive student, or mentally ill person will live will be needed to review the choice of goals. This may be easier to implement in community-based treatment, but is even more necessary in programs where the individual is removed from the community for a time and then returned.

For Whose Benefit?

Representation might help settle the issues of norms—what is tolerated, what is deviant, what is desired—but it still raises the issue of for whose benefit the program is undertaken. The main interest to be served in the choice of program goal must be that of the individual involved. This makes therapeutic sense, for if the individual does not cooperate, the program has little chance of success. One author[4] referred sarcastically to relatives, judges, and police as the true clients of mental hospitals. Alabama Governor George Wallace showed accord with this sentiment in his appeal of a judicial decision that the individual must be considered at least as much as the collective social client of behavior programs; but the appeals court in *Wyatt* found Wallace's notion that the individual was relatively unimportant "constitutionally unacceptable." Thus the individual client's interest must take precedence over that of the collective societal client, whether it be school board, mental health department, law enforcement officers, or concerned citizens.

For the institution's benefit? There are goals that look too far outward toward society and neglect the interest of the individual client. Now we must consider goals that look too far inward and deal only with the client's life in the program or institution. The major problem with such goals is that they do not lead to behavior that will necessarily terminate the state's involvement with the individual or lead to his release from confinement. Many courts have found that the only "treatment," "therapy," or "rehabilitation" that existed in a particular institution was institutional maintenance work.[5] Stories of persons working six or even seven days a week for ten to twelve hours at a time in laundries or other institutional maintenance chores are not unusual.[6] This practice has been called "work therapy" and supposedly shows a person's ability to get back into real life. But experience has shown it may be a fraud. Persons may work for fifteen years at the same job and still be the same. The critical test should be whether the goal of the work assignment is to change a behavior needed to make the individual ready for the termination of the program or to do maintenance work at slave labor rates. The court in *Souder v. Brennan* has answered that the work must be reimbursed at fair wage rates, and this will help avoid needless make-work tasks.[7] But the essential question is still whether the goal is to benefit the individual or the institution. The court in *Wyatt* surveyed three facilities in Alabama and found that treatment plans were "geared to housekeeping functions and continuation of work assignments." They ordered that to stop.

Obviously a work assignment can be a legitimate part of an overall goal, and housekeeping (make your own bed, clean up your room) might be a legitimate part of the work task. But the whole must demonstrably and sequentially lead toward a goal which will mark the end of the program.

Thus the major problem with inward-looking goals is that the real purpose of any program—release of the individual—is too easily forgotten.

A second problem with inward-looking goals is that the thrust of behavior change might be to make the individual adjust to the needs of the institution (for example, to become a "better" prisoner) rather than to adjust to the life he must lead on the outside. It is one thing for an institution to require adherence to certain rules of conduct needed to keep things running. But it is counter-rehabilitative, and should be seen as illegitimate, to try to permanently change behavior toward an institutional adjustment.

For the benefit of researchers? As part of the same line of reasoning, the argument could be made against research performed simply because the subject will be confined long enough to make a good subject for research. In these types of programs, behavior change is undertaken simply to demonstrate the ability of the researcher to engineer change and not toward achieving a central terminal goal. One can certainly allow such research, assuming the full consent of the subject, but only if it does not interrupt or conflict with a continuing program of behavior change calculated to lead to the individual's release. All too often release is contingent, in part, on going along with the administration of the institution, and participation in the research project may be seen as cooperative behavior and as a signal of progress in rehabilitation. But that is far too subjective to be free from abuse. Some institutions apparently see their client population as sitting around with nothing better to do than have research performed on them, and some observers of prisons have suggested there are even monetary reasons for some administrators to push research.[8] The best safeguard against abuse and hidden motives is the concrete, observable goal against which a continuing program can be observed and against which extraneous research and treatment can be seen as irrelevant and therefore unjustified.

Limits on Government Intervention
Is the goal related to the initial problem? Another problem with adopting inward-looking goals is that the reason the individual got into the program in the first place

can be forgotten or neglected. As the Supreme Court has made clear,[9] the nature and duration of the government's involvement must bear a reasonable relation to the purposes for which the state became involved. If an individual's aggressiveness warranted some program of intervention, but the proposed program dealt with many superficial details and did not deal directly with the problem of aggressiveness, then there is a question whether there was any legitimate goal. It is possible that other matters, in addition to the paramount goal, might be dealt with along the way. And an institution does have a duty to maintain order, so that it might engage in needed behavior programs. But the consistently demonstrable thrust of all intervention should be focused on the problem behavior that led to a decision to become involved.

Can the goal be achieved? Another condition on the goal is that it must be achievable. If the program cannot take the individual toward a goal and see it achieved, then the person may be permanently involved in a program. The law is not yet clear on the duration allowable for such a program but it should be clear that the duration must be related to some specific offending behavior (rather than to just a classification or status). If the terminal goal is not achievable, or if when it is achieved it would not justify release from further involvement, then the program could last indefinitely; the law will not tolerate such a program.[10]

The law currently allows indefinite confinement in some cases, but the result is quite unsatisfactory—minimum treatment possibilities and maximum loss of liberty. The growing requirement for adequate treatment and progress toward realizable goals should eventually terminate programs of indefinite duration. If the institution cannot offer an achievable terminal goal, or if the individual does not progress toward that goal in a reasonable period of time, then the obvious alternative is to terminate the program and return the person to his previous environment. If that is impossible because of dangerousness or some other problem, then another social agency might have to accept custody, but you cannot simply keep the person in an indefinite holding pattern until you figure out a successful treatment program.

Dead-end goal-less projects. The requirement that your program progress toward a goal suggests that the law will not tolerate dead-end programs aimed not at changing behavior but rather at getting an individual out of the way. Some critics have recently proposed establishing alternate schools for disruptive students.[11] Some very successful centers [12] have been set up where troubled or troublesome students were sent for behavior change work with the anticipation that, once changed, they would be transferred back to the regular education to which they were entitled. But a former principal of one such center reported that, not surprisingly, the regular school principals did not want them back. The goal of such programs must be to integrate the individual back into the environment. And a court would certainly look past any stated goal to see whether the program was actually detouring persons away from regular services into segregated dead-end goal-less projects.

Individual goals. The changing requirements in the law as to individual treatment programs, as in *Wyatt,* indicate that the goal should be individual. Obviously the number of persons involved, size of staff, physical limitations, and so forth might dictate that individuals with similar goals might be placed together. But two important distinctions must be kept in mind. The grouping must come after an individual determination of goal and treatment plan, not before: An individual should not be placed in a program simply because that is the one available. Second, the progress should not be lock step. As an individual progresses, his program must change; he must not be held back until everyone in the group is ready. Individualized programs are more difficult to create and run, but they are worth it. And the law is beginning to require it. In *Donaldson* one psychiatrist testified that although the patient seemed to be progressing well and was nearing release, he was treated just like the nine hundred other patients. *If a patient is nearing release, he cannot be treated just like all the other patients.* Fifteen years later the patient, still confined, sued and won release and money damages from the psychiatrist.

The goal should be individual; the program should be individual; and the assessment of progress should be individual.

Is the goal positive? The goal of a behavior change program should also be positive. It is fruitless to have as a goal a negative "Don't do that again." If that is the goal, then confinement will probably be successful because it takes away the opportunity to engage in the act, but a behavior change program would be quite artificial. However, if a goal representing some positive behavior incompatible with the offending activity can be suggested, a behavior change program could be developed. There is a big difference between behavior suppression, or control, and behavior change. In the next chapter we will discuss some of the distinctions, but the main one is that a positive goal can be broken down into achievable tasks and progress can be noted toward that goal. A negative goal has only one item of information: Did the person not do "it" again today? It has no subtasks, no skills to be taught—in short no action that can be taken, only suppression. And after the individual is no longer subject to the suppression, and returns to the environment in which he first committed the offending behavior, there is little guarantee he will refrain. In fact, recidivism statistics suggest just the opposite. So from a therapeutic and a legal standpoint a positive goal makes sense.

We have looked at priorities in establishing behavior change goals—a proper behavior change goal reflects community norms, is for the client's benefit, relates to a specific problem behavior, is observable, individual, and positive, and defines the termination point for the behavior change program. We must now examine the substance of the goals.

RANGE OF GOALS
The goal might be to change behavior of employees of the institution or the way in which the institution functions. The need for change does not rest solely with the clients of

our institutions, and, even if the client needs to change, the key may still be in changing staff and institutional behavior. This type of goal is subject to certain challenges (see Chapter 4), but another substantive concern is that goals may be frivolous, improper, so unusual as to jeopardize the program, or even illegal. So just because the program has concrete goals, that does not make it all right.

The goal of one behavior change program in a public institution was to get the women participants to like housework. The reason was that the women had been admitted to the institution partly because of depression which grew out of never-ending household chores, but the goal of learning to like housework could be viewed as frivolous if not downright harmful.

Improper Goals

Some improper or questionable program goals involve sex roles in school and swearing by prison inmates. Eliminating swearing is hardly a goal which would achieve release, nor would it likely be a new behavior maintained after release. As such it seems an improper goal for a behavior change program. Later we will discuss functional skills, and the self-control of swearing would certainly fit in a program to learn skills in dealing with the public, but the control of inmates' language for the institution's benefit is not an appropriate goal.

Another program sought to change behavior in schools if boys seemed to be effeminate or if girls seemed to be adopting male roles. Schools already do so much in teaching sex roles and enforcing sexual stereotypes that Title IX of the 1972 Elementary and Secondary Education Act Amendments [13] forbids them from persisting. Consequently, such a sex role behavior change program for the schools would seem highly improper. A concerned school teacher or counselor could alert a parent and let the parent take it from there.

Unusual Goals

Programs might have an unusual goal which, although

not illegal or even improper, jeopardizes the project. At one state hospital, [14] several males who had sexually assaulted children were discovered in counselor interviews to be homosexual. But they were very unsuccessful homosexuals. The program's hypothesis was that the homosexual finds himself in a hostile environment and must engage in very covert expressions of sexual interest. One who has not learned these social skills will be rebuffed, frustrated, and may turn to sexual offenses. The counselor constructed a voluntary program to have other homosexuals teach these men how to be sufficiently successful that they could satisfy their sexual interests with other homosexuals and thus leave children alone. Program results are not known, but the concept was certainly creative (and in striking contrast to the stereotype behavior change treatment of homosexuals through electric shock). But this goal, for a publicly funded program, was so unusual that one might imagine a legislature denying it funds or a court stating that it was not within the purview of the institution to teach such behavior.

Illegal Goals

Some programs' goals are clearly illegal. Some prison administrators have called for programs to break a prisoner's will or have created programs that really amount to unauthorized punishment. [15] The theory of military basic training suggests that a combination of physical and psychological stress breaks down an individual so that new behaviors can be more easily trained. That is also the layman's conception of "brainwashing." [16] And it seems to be the reality in some American prisons. One goal of the Federal Bureau of Prisons' START project was the warden's explicit demand to break prisoners' spirits. A typical beginning is to get a prisoner to inform on other prisoners. This, according to some wardens, begins a break with the prison subculture, and the tension will sufficiently break the prisoner's spirit and allow him to be remade as loyal to the administration. [17] A good argument could be made that such a goal is unconstitutional. The tasks required to accomplish it are also probably illegal. And the whole effort is hardly therapeutic. The goal is to make the person a manageable prisoner, not a good citizen adjusted to the outside world. In this era we should be wary of those who feel a person is rehabilitated when he will abandon his principles and do anything to be rewarded by his supervisors.

Needless to say, a behavior change specialist should not lend his talents to such an endeavor. And if he chooses to do so, he should not be surprised to be sued by a client asking money damages for a knowing and willful violation of his constitutional rights.

Much more common than these prison programs are efforts in the public schools which seek to enforce disciplinary sanctions that courts have found to be illegal but which school officials still persist in.[18] Behavior change specialists should be wary of compliance in such an enterprise. If you are involved in a school program dealing with children who are "insubordinate" or "disrespectful," you would be well-served to discover what the specific behavior is—it might be something dealing with speech, dress, assembly, publication, or other acts which are protected by law.

Social Goals

Assuming your behavior change goal is justifiable, it will likely fall into one of two areas: social goals or functional skill goals. The former is fraught with problems because it involves the normative cultural judgments discussed earlier. In public schools, a new problem is emerging which has to do with what is generally called "value education."[19] Schools have recently recognized that they teach more than the three R's and that in fact they instill values which children will draw upon throughout life. Confronting this directly, some schools have added value education to their formal curriculum and have run head-on into parents who want to get back to the traditional three R's.

The sentiment of the traditionalists would bar schools, or any state agent from seeking to change the values, beliefs, and attitudes of a student. Language to that effect was contained in the proposed bill on student record privacy, introduced in the United States Senate by Senator James Buckley, but it was deleted on the Senate floor before final passage. [20] Had the language been retained, it is doubtful whether most school counselors or behavior change practitioners in schools could continue to operate without constant legal scrutiny. A similar bill was introduced in Maryland[21] and if passed would probably have the same effect. So if your goal is in the social/cultural area, filled with value judgments as to what is desired or appropriate conduct, then you must keep abreast of legislative changes.

Functional Skills

The area of functional skills is much easier to define and to defend. A typical program would be to teach social communications skills to a withdrawn mental patient, to teach a prisoner confined for assault to control his temper and substitute verbal assertiveness for physical assault, or to teach a failing, disruptive student to successfully complete tasks. The list of similar programs is very long. This is a very promising approach, because establishing a goal in a framework of specific functional skills and then creating a learning structure to teach them is probably the most hopeful way to treat many people in our prisons, hospitals, and schools. Work by behavioral scientists is being documented in a wide range of programs, and usable data about relative effectiveness of this approach will be available in the coming years.

CHAPTER 5 REVIEW CHECKLIST

1. Does your program have a concrete, objectively stated goal?

2. Is it directly related to the reason the individual was brought to your attention?

3. When it is achieved, can your involvement with the client be terminated?

4. Will the change benefit the individual more than the institution?

5. Can the goal be achieved?

6. Is the goal a positive behavior change rather than a negative behavior suppression?

7. Does the goal involve changing a behavior that is actually constitutionally permissible?

6

Motivating Behavior Change

SUMMARY

Your approach must include techniques for actually motivating behavior change in order to meet legal requirements for treatment. Traditional psychotherapies may not be effective enough to meet this test. Aversive motivation strategies might be attempted only after less drastic alternatives have failed. Structured learning approaches must not manipulate, as rewards, items to which clients are entitled as a right. Chapter 6 outlines the characteristics of various therapeutic approaches that motivate sufficiently to meet legal minimum requirements, but which do not raise additional legal problems in the process.

GENERAL MOTIVATION STRATEGIES

When a person is confined, the *quid pro quo* for allowing confinement, according to *Donaldson,* is treatment sufficient to qualify the person for release. But how do you motivate someone to change his behavior? It should be expected that courts and administrative bodies overseeing the protection of this newly emerging constitutional right to individual treatment would favor motivation schemes 1) that present detailed treatment programs, 2) that meet the counselor:client ratio problem by enlisting clients, staff, and outsiders as paraprofessional aides, 3) that can document progress, 4) that require only a short period, and 5) the effects of which last for a long time.

With these requirements in mind, we can examine three general types of strategies: traditional types of therapy, aversive forces, and structured learning situations. We can omit, from this discussion of motivation, areas such as psychosurgery and electrical stimulation of the brain because they are done *to* individuals, rather than relying on the individual to be motivated to do something himself.

Traditional Therapies

Traditional therapies, particularly nondirective psychoanalytic group activities, may not meet the constitutionally required level of treatment adequacy. In *Morales,* drawing on *Donaldson* and *Wyatt,* the court suggested that group programs, in which individuals were not attended to, were not sufficient. Thus group therapies common in prisons and mental institutions must be more than just "milieu therapy" in order to be treatment. Individuals could certainly be treated in a group—so long as they each have an individual treatment plan—but not if they are simply left to do whatever the group as a whole seems to require.

Nondirectional techniques which are individual and thus seem to escape the group treatment burden may still fail for lack of an adequately defined program. Can a psychoanalyst really file a program for individual treatment with the expectation that the real problem will be uncovered and that the client will gain needed insight and correct his behavior? It is not clear whether the highly personal nature of psychoanalysis will be able to meet the need for clear program design.

Does it work? Courts will likely begin to require data on results of various treatment approaches (largely focusing on length of average time required for treatment, and success in changing behaviors) and also raise questions of practicality. In one reported case[1] a therapist was responsible for as many as nine hundred individuals. Individual psychoanalysis may simply not be believable in that case. But if you want to practice intensive psychoanalysis with a few patients and leave the rest to "milieu therapy" you may be prohibited from doing so.

Schools must motivate. A similar problem exists in schools and other social agencies. If a student were confined to a special program, he could not simply be allowed to stay there until he decides to shape up. The *quid pro quo* for allowing different treatment is precisely a treatment program calculated to get the client back into the mainstream. And a necessary element of such a program would be a motivation scheme.

Schools have been guilty of creating programs in which a troublesome student is transferred to a dead-end school where he can simply be left to languish. Many schools also faced handicapped children with either a minimum offer of services and little attempt to motivate them to do more, or an outright exclusion of services because such handicapped children could presumably not use them. The right to education cases such as *PARC* and *Mills* show that services offered must be offered to all. Children cannot be tracked off into other programs, as in *Hobson,* and there must be an attempt to motivate them.

The main step taken to meet this new requirement of treatment has been "mainstreaming," and federal regulations and many state legislatures now require that all clients of a service be together and that any peripheral program's goal must be to get their clients in the mainstream. Ironically, this reform, which seems the logical antidote to both tracking and exclusion, might now be challenged for not being enough[2] or allowing the situation to worsen.[3] I have seen retarded children in the mainstream of an open space school, and the promising reform seems to turn into a cruel joke because the children cannot read or work independently or interact with their peers. The spirit of *Donaldson-Wyatt-Morales* might be applied to suggest that "mainstreaming" the retarded might be just as hollow as "milieu therapy" for patients and prisoners.

The challenge is thus great for those providing psychological services to schools. Children cannot be segregated into special programs unless the specific intent is to raise them to a functional level where they can re-enter the mainstream; but if kept in the mainstream, students needing special treatment must receive individual assistance. The need to train teachers, parents, and other students to aid in the behavior change program is already a practical necessity in most schools and may become a legal requirement.

Drugs do not motivate. A similar problem faces the use
of drugs used in traditional therapy to change behavior. As
data become available which show that drugs may only
mask behavior, and that they may lose their potency after a
while, the case might be better made that they are not really
"treatment." Conversely, as information becomes available
that there *are* ways to treat hyperactivity in children or depression in adults (two large targets for drugs) without medical
intervention, the requirement might be made that these
alternatives be pursued first and that drugs be used only if
other means fail.

Aversive Forces

The second major grouping of motivational techniques
includes aversive forces—punishment applied in a way intended to change behavior. The behavioral principles relied
on are the deceptively simple ones of negative reinforcement
and aversive conditioning.

Operant conditioning: Negative reinforcement. In negative reinforcement, drawing on principles of operant (or
Skinnerian) conditioning, an unpleasant event is terminated as
soon as the individual stops doing some behavior, and he is
thus negatively reinforced for stopping. In a natural environment there are many opportunities for such behavior shaping,
but the legal problem arises when the unpleasant event is
artificially introduced to change behavior.

This is the lame justification for such punishment as was
carried out in *Morales.* After someone engages in an undesired behavior, an unpleasant task is assigned, such as a
painful work detail, or outright punishment, such as tear
gassing, is administered. The theory is that such an aversive
force will teach the individual "not to do it again," thus
changing behavior for the better. The technique is ancient,
but the new behavioral jargon has been adopted by some; the
Morales court was told that what appears to be senseless, mali-
cious harassment of juveniles is "behavioral modification."

These attempts at use of aversion, then, are not really
based on negative reinforcement but are pure punishment,

hardening behaviors rather than teaching new ones, and inspiring more undesired behaviors. As a California court observed,[4] "The type of confinement depicted. . . results in a slow-burning fire of resentment on the part of the inmates until it finally explodes in open revolt, coupled with their violent and bizarre conduct."

It is not the intent of this chapter to catalog all the abuses which are perpetrated in the name of this discredited notion that punishment is an effective way to change behavior.

Even newer, more sophisticated uses of aversive force will not work in an institution. For the behavioral scientist to be satisfied that the application had a theoretical chance of succeeding, the unpleasant stimulus would have to be presented as soon as the undesired behavior begins and then terminated immediately upon the cessation of the undesired behavior. That is impossible in the context of an institution like a prison, mental hospital, or school. Much time will likely pass between a behavior such as an infraction of some rule and the carrying out of punishment—too much time to activate the behavioral principle. With such a lapse of time, what is really punished is not so much the behavior as it is getting caught. In fact, there may be intervening desirable behavior. If a behavior change program sought to solve this problem by instituting a more immediate aversive consequence, there would be a legal problem. Due process requirements may call for at least a hearing and possibly a chance to appeal before the punishment is administered. For severe punishments, certainly anything corporal, these requirements would produce a lengthy delay.

So the use of punishment as part of a negative reinforcement scheme to change behavior is too ineffective to meet the constitutional standards for treatment. It can only be explained as an attempt to temporarily suppress behavior in order to serve the institution's need; it certainly has no place in a formal behavior change program.

Respondent conditioning: Aversive treatment. The second type of aversive motivation relies on a notion of respondent (or Pavlovian) conditioning which is quite frightening to laymen. It is the stuff of the movie *A Clockwork Orange* and gives the impression that a person can, against his will, be permanently and unalterably changed. The data do not show either large results or long-lasting change but that should not make the involuntary administration of this therapy less threatening or more acceptable.

The typical forms of aversive conditioning used in public institutions are drug-induced nausea or respiratory paralysis, and electric shock (which differs from electroconvulsive therapy). The theoretical concept is apparently that an aversive stimulus (drug or shock) can be paired with a behavior until it conditions a physiological involuntary response; and that in the future the behavior, or even thinking about it, will produce the same response.

The most serious legal questions about this form of therapy involve consent and safeguards against abuse. Several California prisoners who had undergone therapy with drugs which simulate respiratory failure commented that it was the worst experience of their lives.[5] One could hardly expect them to consent to repeat it. Following the reasoning in *Kaimowitz* a court might wonder whether anyone in an institution might consent. And without that consent, it would certainly be barred. The lower court in *Wyatt* found a right to be free from "adversive (sic) reinforcement conditioning" absent consent, and as this is interpreted by other courts it might provide a broad prohibition against the use of force.

A second legal problem, partly motivating the court in *Wyatt,* was the lack of safeguards against abuse. The administering of the aversive treatment might be indistinguishable from unauthorized punishment. There is no automatic safeguard against staff calling proscribed punishment "aversive therapy" and going ahead with it. Although there seems to be no test for making the distinction at the time, a court can probably determine in retrospect if that were the case. If the stimulus were used repeatedly over a long period of time, ostensibly to change the same behavior, then it is certainly not effective therapy but is only unauthorized punishment.

Electric shock. One form of aversive therapy *does* seem to be effective but often faces legal challenges—the use of electric shock with retarded or autistic children who display self-injurious behavior, such as head-banging, biting, or digging nails into flesh. The theoretical basis for the therapy is that by pairing a slight aversive stimulus with each incident of such behavior, it can be stopped.

More important, for legal requirements, the previously self-stimulating child may now begin to react to external stimuli, thus making effective therapy a possibility. So the test should be that aversive therapy might be used where other therapy has not worked, where it can be administered to save the individual from immediate and continuing self-injury, when it allows freedom from physical restraints which would otherwise be continued, when it can be administered for only a few short instances, and when its goal is to make other nonaversive therapy possible. Such an aversive program certainly requires consent from a guardian and immediate review of the results of *each separate administration.*[6]

Structured Learning versus
Traditional Rewards and Punishment

The final group of motivational techniques involves structured learning experiences. These are often seen simplistically as "giving rewards for good behavior," and therefore seem similar to traditional institutional techniques. It is ironic whenever behavior change programs, particularly "behavior modification," are criticized for using external rewards and punishments to manipulate behavior, because virtually all our institutions have been doing that, with questionable success, for years.

Traditional rewards in prisons. Prisons traditionally use time off for good behavior, work-release, jobs with pay, conjugal visits, parole, trusty status with various privileges, and other incentives as rewards. They use techniques such as "the hole," removal of various privileges, beatings, and adding time to the sentence as punishments.

So reward and punishment is not new—but in its traditional use it does not teach behavior. Rewards are dispensed in the absence of bad behavior; punishments occur for what is perceived as bad behavior. But there is no consequence for learning a new behavior. It is as if the institution were established not to help people get better but just to see that they do not get worse.[7]

One innovation seemed aimed at a more sophisticated use of rewards—the indeterminate sentence. The theory was that once a prisoner had demonstrated rehabilitation he would be released: Commitments to mental institutions are implicitly indeterminate sentences. The abuses have been terrible, with administrators and therapists able to play with a man's liberty like a yo-yo, taunting him with release to freedom and then keeping him locked up for any of a wide range of unreviewable subjective judgments. People have typically spent much longer time behind bars on an indeterminate sentence than the maximum they would have served on a fixed one.[8]

These problems probably occur because the single reward—freedom—is not directly related to any steps an inmate can take to lead to that goal. Consequently, it provides no traceable motivation. In Virginia prisons a proposal that would tie release directly to specific tasks to be performed and that would contract for release upon successful performance has been discussed. If the tasks were relevant to the reason for confinement, that might be a worthy reform. But it would still require having an indeterminate sentence, and that flexibility may be severely limited in the future. This is just another example of a "reform" which is promising in theory, intolerable in practice, and apparently nearing suicide by abuse.

Traditional rewards in mental institutions. Traditional methods of motivation in mental institutions also seem like simply structured reward and punishment. As patients seem able, they might mingle with others in their building, then be allowed to stroll the grounds, then to work for pay in the institution, then to leave the grounds on supervised outings, then to leave unsupervised, then to work outside, then to live outside, and finally to be discharged. Conversely, as rules are broken, or for other presumably therapeutic reasons, these activities would be limited.

This system seems to provide motivation—but for what? If the goal is to motivate behavior change then it apparently is not met. Research on the difficulties that persons leaving mental institutions face and data on the high percentage that return to the institution indicate that needed behaviors are not learned.[9] So what behavior *is* motivated by these traditional reward and punishment schemes? The inmates learn what *not* to do, and how to either adjust to the rules of the institution or escape detection when breaking rules. What is being taught is docility, secretiveness, and even withdrawal. So the motivators traditionally used may actually explain the inability of many inmates to adjust to the outside.

School rewards. Schools also use traditional rewards and punishments to attempt to motivate students. Rewards include grades, gold stars, special honors programs, skipping a grade, good recommendations from teachers, field trips, and eventual release through graduation. Punishments include bad grades, trips to the principal's office, threats, corporal punishment, notes home to parents, failure, transfer to a special program, suspension, and expulsion. Any observer of the modern classroom knows that this system is not structured in a way that consistently motivates good behavior. In fact, with petty theft, drug use, vandalism, truancy, and assault on the increase, either the traditional motivators are having no impact or they are reinforcing the wrong type of behavior.

Although prisons, schools, and mental institutions draw upon large varieties of rewards and punishments, they seem to ignore them as prime instruments of motivation because of two beliefs. First, they believe that a person should be internally rather than externally motivated—that people ought to want to do a thing for its own sake. Second, as a corollary, when a person actually *does* something, the person is expected to be motivated by that performance and not by anything external such as praise or other social reinforcers.

Researchers in behavioral science have strongly suggested that such internal motivation is preferable, if it exists; but if it does not, then to presume it does means the institution's motivation plan rests on a moral exhortation, not on a scientific reality.[10] To meet the growing requirement that there be adequate individual treatment, institutions must assure that there is a motivation strategy being employed for a particular individual which moves him toward his individual goal. This is part of any behavior change program and cannot be neglected.

STRUCTURED LEARNING: POSITIVE MOTIVATION STRATEGIES

We might group positive motivation strategies in three types: social, tangible, and token and tier systems.

Social Motivation

Social motivations draw upon the reinforcing verbal and nonverbal behaviors of others in the client's social environment. But rather than leaving them to chance, they are designed along the lines of the structured learning techniques detailed in Chapter 4—providing positive reinforcement as skills are practiced and shaped to a desired level of performance.

Two examples might be useful. In one state prison, an inmates' council assessed the main reasons why released inmates returned to prison. One was that they would be harassed about being an ex-con and would hit someone. Another reason was that they would join with old friends and get involved in some escapade that would eventually end in breaking the law. The traditional motivators—an opportunity to be released from confinement and warnings not to break the law again—did not help. A program was begun in which models showed how to react to taunts about being an ex-convict and to invitations from old friends to join in some escapade. In role-playing sessions inmates practiced the modeled skills, learning how to control their tempers, how to respond with verbal repartee rather than physical force, and how to say "no" to friends without losing face. In the process they became less sensitive and thus less easily provoked. There is no longitudinal data on this approach but logic certainly commends it.

In several state mental institutions, inmates are being moved rapidly out of the hospitals (largely for economic reasons) and back into the community. But they often lack skills needed to function effectively. Some programs [11] specify skills needed for social and vocational effectiveness and for reintegration into family life. These skills are modeled and role-played in client group sessions where approximation toward successful performance is reinforced. Clients then do "homework" in the community and bring their experiences back to following sessions so that specifically needed skills and levels of performance can be determined, modeled, role-played, and achieved before the voluntary program is terminated.

Tangible Rewards

For some persons neither the internal feeling of accomplishment nor the external social reinforcement will be enough to get things going. A counselor cannot simply sit on his hands and wish for motivation—the emerging right to treatment demands that he find a motivating force. That force may be the personal impact of the therapist, or the dynamics of a group setting, but if nothing in the social environment moves the client, you must. In such cases, external tangible rewards must be contemplated. Tangible rewards might include food, activities, and even money.

Tangibles might be administered in a one-to-one treatment setting, which is undoubtedly best. The initial problem is to decide what will motivate the individual, and that decision is best made by the individual himself. In a one-to-one situation another important advantage is that the reward can be delivered immediately, and the client can take the time right then to enjoy his reward. This is important not only logistically but also because the social interaction in giving the reward can lead to a phasing out of the tangible and a building up of the social reinforcement. And, as an individual's tastes change, different rewards can be instituted.

Tokens and Tiers

In most situations in public institutions you must deal with groups, and a token system offers several advantages. [12] Rather than having to select individual tangible rewards for each group member, the members can pick from a menu of reinforcers. And rather than actually delivering each reward as it is earned, a token can be given immediately. This provides the immediate feedback so often needed to make the event motivating; and by needing to save tokens to redeem for larger rewards a client can learn the virtues of delayed gratification.

The tokens may be used in a dynamic program providing individual treatment for each client, or they may be frozen in a more static arrangement like a tier system. [13] In a typical tier arrangement, the entire environment is the reward. At one level there is a certain type of room, bed, clothing, food, personal property, access to TV and other recreational facilities, hours for visitation, educational and vocational programs, hygienic facilities, and even some degree of privacy. As a person earns tokens and progresses up the tier, everything gets better—a better bed, more visitors, opportunities for programs, and so forth. The theory is simple—the better grades of environment provide the motivation to do what is necessary to progress. And that is the first problem—what is necessary? Generally in a tier the behaviors to be rewarded are non-behaviors, such as avoiding infractions. Sometimes they are highly questionable behaviors such as informing on fellow clients. The tokens needed for a better environment may be awarded upon the acquisition of specific behaviors, but most likely they are awarded simply upon the passage of time with a group moving lock step to the next tier. Thus no particular behavior is taught, and no particular behavior is reinforced. The severity of punishment is also not necessarily related to a specific behavior because it requires, in a tier system, removing a whole range of tangible reinforcers at once, bouncing the person down a few tiers.

This tier approach is not at all unlike systems which have been used for many years in prisons, mental institutions, and residential schools, with clients grouped at various levels. In fact upon examination some behavior change programs have appeared to be only the status quo disguised in new language. But courts are not buying it, and tier systems in public institutions might be dropped or banned entirely in the near future because of the convergence of three features.

Possible abuse. First is the question of abuse. Allowing vital parts of the environment to be manipulated by poorly trained and possibly antagonistic staff presents too much potential for abuse to be tolerated.[14] It is not important how the plan looked on the drawing board or how well the staff training session seemed to go. The important thing is what happened once the program was turned over to the staff. I have observed classrooms in which point sheets were turned in by students eagerly working to earn rewards, and the sheets were destroyed by aides who did not like a particular child. We have also heard of situations in mental institutions in which staff were supposed to give tokens for communicative speech and ignore babbling, but they instead simply rewarded patients they liked and ignored patients they did not want to interact with. In prisons there are reports of antagonistic guards adding and subtracting points for very subjective judgments scarcely related to any program goals. Thus the potential for abuse is very great.

Effectiveness. A second reason for attacking tier and token systems is that they just do not work effectively. Current constitutional requirements demand individual treatment that motivates an individual toward an individual goal. Tier programs offer group treatment that does not motivate and which often has a goal that benefits primarily the institution, not the client. As the federal court in *Morales* stated, ". . . behavior modification through the use of point systems (does not) rise to the dignity of professional treatment programs geared to individual juveniles." As standards of adequacy are strengthened, the use of tier systems will probably decrease. The more individualized the token system, the fewer problems it will face.

Rights vs. privileges. But the third and strongest objection to the use of tier systems is that they often involve the deprivation of items to which an individual is entitled as a right. Courts have only recently laid down certain minimum rights in mental institutions and prisons.[15] The significance of this lies in drawing a line where a tier system can begin and below which it cannot drop. In some programs the beginning level may be only one meal a day, no daily showers, no privacy, only institutional clothing or perhaps no clothing at all, no daily exercise, no visitors including clergy and attorneys, no mail in or out, no personal belongings such as reading material, and so forth. The system is supposed to arrange the volume and frequency with which such items could be enjoyed and use that for motivation. What really happens is a type of aversive stimulation—inmates behave a certain way to escape or avoid severe deprivation.

An interesting philosophical question is raised. Can using such extreme measures be justified in terms of speeding an inmate toward his freedom, and is this preferable to kindly custodial care that leaves him unchanged and thus confined? But the question no longer belongs in the theoretical realm—it is being answered by courts and legislatures. Lengthy portions of the opinions in *Wyatt* and *Morales* detail the minimum rights to be accorded as a matter of constitutional right. Behavior change specialists can no longer manipulate basic items in the environment and call them privileges to be earned, for they are rights, not privileges.

This does not mean that programs cannot be built around the way in which items are made available. For example, everyone must receive a nutritionally adequate meal, but some persons might earn a special dessert. In one program involving children, everyone got the same lunch, but children competed for the privilege of being first in line. You cannot deny a person access to a common room which might have a television set, but some corrections programs have arranged tasks by which a prisoner can earn a television set for his own room.[16] In all these cases basic items were being provided as required, but with creativity they were made to work as a motivating force.

Some behaviorists argue that some mental patients do not respond to any reinforcers except sleeping and eating, and unless those can be manipulated, the therapist will be denied the tools he needs, the client will be denied effective aid, and the institution will fail to meet its duty to treat. That argument loses its force when it is repeated by every experimenter trying to push his own brand of therapy. Practitioners advocating psychosurgery, electrical stimulation of the brain, electroconvulsive therapy, electric shock, and drugs all argue that unless they have their way, the client will be denied effective treatment.

The law will no longer tolerate manipulation of basic needs because, in the past, such programs have always sunk to the lowest allowable level and attempted to motivate everyone in that way. The therapist who can show a Human Rights Committee or a court a specific individual who has not responded to any less restrictive alternative can probably win a chance to restrict meals for a few days. But if it does not produce some results within a very short time, such as forty-eight hours, then it will certainly be discontinued.

TIME OUT
A final motivational technique bears some comments. It follows that if the client is in a motivating environment, whether it is one he enjoys intrinsically or one which provides him external rewards, he will want to remain in that environment. Conversely, being removed from that environment can motivate him to want to do something to return and to avoid doing something that will remove him again. Social reinforcement strategists have experimented with this concept of "Time Out" from a reinforcing environment. [17] And behavior change specialists suggest that it is the most humane form of punishment since it is simply the absence of reward.[18]

But it contains a real potential for abuse in institutional settings. It involves isolation which seems to provide a therapeutic justification for throwing a prisoner in "the hole," or locking away a troublesome mental patient, or placing a person on the bottom tier level where he receives no rewards. It is hard to monitor length of time in Time Out. It is supposed to last only a few minutes, but I have seen mental institution inmates taken to their room for Time Out and then forgotten for hours by an overworked aide.

The *Morales* case should end this kind of problem. Judge William Wayne Justice declared that isolation for disciplinary reasons was a sufficiently severe deprivation of liberty that it required due process procedures. This means that in advance of the isolation there must be notice of intent to discipline, a period of time to allow the inmate to prepare a defense, and a hearing. Obviously, the theoretical basis for Time Out could not be served by this delay so the technique might as well be discarded. Judge Justice also requires that during isolation the inmate must be visited at least each hour [19]—an understandable safeguard against just forgetting the person. But it also cuts into the theoretical concept, because the prison psychiatrist stopping in to see the person every hour could be more reinforcing than the environment from which the person was removed.

Judge Justice recognizes that some forms of behavior modification are so mild that they do not warrant the full due process procedures, and the use of a minute or two of Time Out would certainly fit within that constraint. So if your program can assure that any administration of Time Out as a motivating technique will not stretch to an hour or otherwise represent a substantial deprivation of liberty, then it might be used. If you cannot make that guarantee, then it should not even be attempted.

CHAPTER 6 REVIEW CHECKLIST

1. Do you have a strategy to motivate the individual client toward some specific goal?

2. Can you show effectiveness data on use of the strategy with similar clients?

3. Do you periodically review progress to check the effectiveness of the motivation strategy?

4. If you use aversive strategies, can you show that you tried less drastic alternatives first, that they were ineffective, and that the aversive strategy will work?

5. Could you explain to a court, in terms of effectiveness, the difference between your aversive strategy and punishment?

6. Is your structured learning approach really a treatment technique or just the traditional system of rewards and punishments operating in the institutional environment?

7. If you use tokens, do you have an individualized program?

8. Do you use as rewards things which the client should receive as a matter of right?

9. If a person fails to earn tokens, or begins at the basic tier level, is the client in a state of deprivation below that allowed by law?

10. If you use Time Out, do you have safeguards to assure it can only be used for a few minutes?

7

Contractual Problems

SUMMARY

Many behavior change programs are undertaken by consultants to public agencies, but agencies may lack authority to contract out certain behavior change responsibilities because of constitutionally mandated duties or agreements with persons already performing services. The consultant's approach should be unique enough to justify using outside help, yet be able to be taught to staff members, so that outside help must not be permanently employed. The consultant cannot so completely take over, however, that there would be an illegal delegation of authority or of policy-making functions. These are the questions that must be raised to determine if a proposed consulting contract will be valid.

CONTRACTUAL PROCEDURE

The world of behavior change specialists is a world of consulting. Even those who are full-time employees in one capacity will often be available for consulting with other public or private agencies. When offered consulting work the specialist usually does not inquire into the authority of the institution to contract for such services, but it would be wise if he did. And the managers of projects contracting for outside help must ask not only whether they can do so within their budget but also whether they can do so within their authority.

The potential danger involved in an abuse of contracting authority is less to the client (he may be well served by the extra help) than to the professional. A project which is terminated midway because of contractual irregularities can interrupt research, can cause an agency to avoid similar

89

projects in the future, and can cause misleading publicity. A school behavior modification project in a Washington suburb two years ago involved a contract, with a private firm, which was deemed by the school board attorney to exceed contracting authority. Headlines in the local newspapers read "Behavior Modification Held Illegal"[1] and to this day school authorities think there was some illegality in the substance of the program rather than in the contracting procedure.

A final reason for attention to contract procedural detail is that innovative approaches *do* find opponents, and they may seize on a contract problem as a weak link. I consulted with an experimental school project in Seattle which faced some potential contractual difficulties. When the major opponent of the program was asked why he had not exploited these problems, he replied that the project would be given a chance to fail and that only if it succeeded would it be stopped in court. The predictable publicity would be that the approach was faulty, and it would probably not be tried again.

Thus while you have done your scientific homework in designing what might be a fine project, if someone has not done some legal homework that project may be in jeopardy. The vast majority of contracts are not taken to court and most people need not fear judicial scrutiny. But innovative human services will always trigger opposition—and that is certainly the environment in which contracts are taken to court.

Initial Restrictions

The duty to provide services. The first question is whether the public institution has the authority to contract with behavior change specialists to undertake the particular activity. Courts have held that some services can easily be contracted out; for example, a school can contract out for janitorial services. The reason is that the school is not under a constitutional mandate to provide janitorial services, and such services are procured really for administrative convenience. But where an institution does have a duty to perform a specific function

90

there is less flexibility in contracting out for it. Otherwise it might appear that the institution is avoiding the duty or placing a low priority on it. If a school, for example, contracted out the instruction of all handicapped children, making it necessary for those children to be at a separate facility, a court would likely consider the contract a thinly veiled attempt to segregate those students. So the behavior change specialist must take care that by the nature of his contractual relationship, or the grouping of participants in a project, he is not perpetuating a system which legislatures or courts have sought to alter. As the law changes in regard to new duties (for example, the duty to educate all handicapped children) and as the law clarifies what existing duties mean (what is really required to "treat" or "rehabilitate"), then the flexibility to contract out in those areas may also change.

Present staff. There may also be restrictions on the authority to contract out if there are public employees already hired to perform a similar function. If the intent of the contract is to enable the institution's management to bypass existing staff, then management may have exceeded their authority. However, for economic reasons it is unlikely that existing staff could be simply ignored and a duplicate staff contracted out.

Existing contracts. A third restriction may be imposed by other contracts already negotiated. In some public employee negotiations, the contract will stipulate that some services are to be provided solely by the public employees and are not to be contracted out. This is for the obvious reason that it gives the employees real leverage in determining the future direction of social services. An outside agent being contracted with should not assume that his proposed contract does not conflict with other negotiated agreements. I have seen contracts in several states between school boards and teacher unions which were violated by subsequent contracts with private educational corporations.

Thus the authority to contract may be limited by the duty to provide certain services, persons already hired to perform those services, or existing contracts.

Service Must Be Unique

The test for allowing outside contracts has usually been the unique nature of services which would otherwise not be available to the institution. If what an outside agent proposes to do could just as easily be taught to existing staff by someone inside the institution then there may be little that is unique in that service and little justification for contracting out. Similarly, even if only he can do the job, there may be a training requirement so that the approach can be "turnkeyed" at the end of your project—that is, that staff can be taught to perform the service and continue it afterward. Without this requirement it would appear that the public entity was locking itself into a lifelong need to contract out, and public policy would be better served by a training requirement in the contract. This requirement would likely be welcomed by behavior change specialists using structured learning approaches, for they often want to involve everyone in the program anyway. It does impose quite a burden on other types of behavior change technologies that are highly personal and cannot be taught to aides.

A similar training requirement may arise out of demands by public employees for a greater share in the work of the institution. For example, at several hospitals, striking nurses recently demanded an opportunity to perform more than menial functions. Some public employee unions have already used behavioral training to upgrade paraprofessionals in hospitals, and that kind of technique is likely to be increasingly demanded. This type of training requirement would involve a sharing of responsibilities which is very possible under structured learning technologies but is much less possible with behavior change techniques that rely on medical interventions or other psychoanalytic strategies which cannot be shared with aides.

Excessive Delegation of Authority

A more basic problem with the authority to contract is whether the nature of the relationship delivers so much power to an outside entity that it is therefore illegal. Public institutions are agents of the state. Since they receive their power by delegation, they cannot further dilute the state's authority by turning around and subdelegating it.

Some behavior change specialists have proposed taking over an entire school and running it on a behavior modification basis. Such a project was tried in Indiana in 1970, but appeared to that state's Attorney General to be an excessive grant of authority.[2] In other instances, outside entities have taken over one or two school classrooms.[3] In one county near Washington, D.C., a contract with a private entity to take over several classrooms of disruptive students was declared illegal.[4] The school board attorney found too much authority had passed from the state-created school district, which had limited authority to contract, to an outside entity.

Final Considerations

Funding restrictions? Two other problems may limit the authority to contract. The first is the funding source. Money from the federal government often has legislative restrictions such as "no funds appropriated under this title shall pass to individuals or to profit-making agencies, etc." Such funds are often treated locally as if they were unrestricted, but you should check to make sure your project will not be terminated midway because of some irregularity of this sort.

Related to the institution's goal? A final restriction on authority to contract involves the purpose of the venture. The service should relate to the discharge of the public function which the institution performs. Does a prison have the authority in its charter to contract with a drug company to test experimental drugs on prisoners? This has not yet been decided in the negative by the courts, but a contract for research or treatment that is too unrelated to the work of the institution should not be established.

ILLEGAL DELEGATION OF POLICY-MAKING

Assuming that the public body does have the authority to contract, there is still a potential problem if the arrangement delegates too much policy-making. For example, there may be authority for a school to contract with an outside entity to run a program with disruptive students and train teachers in the technique, but the school must still set the policy guidelines which govern the project. If they were to turn it over to the private entity entirely, it would be as if they were saying, "Take care of these troublemakers for a while and we don't care what you do to them." That would be an excessive grant of policy-making authority and probably would not be allowed.

The test is whether the institution plans to act upon what is learned in the program. In a situation in Texas in which a private educational firm was using behavioral techniques to increase motivation of underachieving students, the Attorney General issued an opinion[5] indicating that the test of policy control was whether the purpose of the undertaking was to inform the public body so that it could adopt successful new approaches. This is welcome leverage, for the corollary should be that the public body would have to act upon favorable results.

A final delegation problem is that for the public body to truly retain control it must be competent to participate in planning, to exercise some discretion during the program, and to evaluate the results. Otherwise they would be so dependent on the outside specialist's evaluation that their policy role would be eroded. This, then, is another opportunity for a training function. Staff and even board members can be taught enough about structured learning approaches to participate vigorously during planning and implementation and to be able to challenge the results.

There are other contractual problems which any outside agent will face in seeking to carry out research or treatment, but they are not dealt with here since they do not affect behavior change projects specifically as opposed to other kinds of projects.

CHAPTER 7 REVIEW QUESTIONS

1. Does the agency have the authority to contract for the service to be provided by the behavior change specialist?

2. Would the contract cause an illegal bypass of public employees already hired?

3. Do the terms of the proposed consulting relationship conflict with existing contracts for services?

4. Is the service unique enough to justify outside assistance, or could existing staff simply teach themselves?

5. Is so much authority delegated to the behavior change specialist that it is illegal?

6. Is the agency's authority to contract limited by guidelines from another body providing funds for the project?

7. Does the contract require the behavior change specialist to usurp the agency's policy-making functions?

8. Does the contract provide for the behavior change specialist to train staff and supervisors in the techniques so that they can fully retain control during planning and implementation?

8

Accountability: Compliance and Effectiveness

SUMMARY

Recent advances in client rights may be lost in our non-accountable self-perpetuating public institutions. The basic behavioral model offers a workable system for increasing compliance with legal changes and effectiveness of treatment: concrete goals, sequenced tasks, feedback on progress, and rewarding desired performance. Institutions might consider contracting out demonstration projects to see how new approaches work before they are unleashed in institutions. New tools are needed to audit the ways public programs affect behavior whether in traditional institutions or in innovative approaches. A system of accountability makes it possible to trace the impact of a behavior change project or a judicial decision, thereby lessening practitioner liability *and* increasing chances for effective treatment.

NONACCOUNTABLE INSTITUTIONS

There is no system of accountability overseeing administration of our public institutions. Their workings are governed and motivated by patterns that have developed over the years in a kind of bureaucratic Darwinism: Behavior which protects the institution and perpetuates its existence is self-rewarding.

Most institutions protect themselves by assuring a lack of information. In virtually any public institution the goals are too imprecise to serve as a standard against which to judge the workings of the institution. It is impossible to tell by whom important decisions will be made, when they will be made, and what factors will be weighed in the process. Once a decision is made, it is impossible to trace its impact, good or bad. There is not only no feedback within the institution, but also no communication of objective data to the public.

The risk of introducing any innovative technique is very great if the institution is not accountable for what is done. Conversely, it is almost a waste to conduct experiments and research in such an institution because the results can never be compared to anything and no results will be acted upon. Thus for a behavior change technology to be practiced without abuse and with the greatest opportunity to realize its full potential, there must be a system of accountability in public institutions. The interests of the law also require such a system if the law is to see that there is compliance with new mandates and effectiveness of treatment.

Compliance is necessary if any new executive guideline, judicial decision, or legislative mandate is to be carried out. How can a nonaccountable institution comply? Worse, how can the executive, judicial, or legislative body know if compliance is occurring? Otherwise, new standards of care won through the legislature may be lowered in practice, and new protections won through judicial battles may not be put into effect. Earlier portions of this book discuss new rights to education or treatment. Defining these rights is futile if no one can tell whether institutions are complying.

A second concern of the law is effectiveness. Underlying every effort of a public institution is the implied notion that it will work effectively, will spend appropriated funds effectively, will train staff effectively, and deliver the most effective treatment. This goes hand in hand with the notion of compliance, for there would be little value in complying with the letter of a mandate while providing an inadequate service. So if the law is to have any impact in regulating behavior change there must be visible compliance and visible effectiveness—an accountable system. The behavioral sciences, whether drawing on systems analysis or organization development, or analogizing from structured learning, offer a workable model.

PROGRESS TOWARD A GOAL:
VISIBLE COMPLIANCE AND EFFECTIVENESS

First, the institution must have goals. Actions not directly related to any goal cannot be judged as either worthwhile or pointless.

Second, those goals must be concrete. They must be something actual and realizable, not just platitudinous statements such as "the best education offered in the nation."

Third, goals must be visible. There must be no disputing whether they are being attained.

Fourth, each goal must be objectively stated so that professional, administrator, legislator, client, parent, and judge can all be using the same language and agree on the results.

Fifth, each goal must be divided into a sequence of tasks. Without subtasks there can be no measure of progress; evaluation would have to wait until the total goal was reached. And without a sequence of steps toward a goal no one could tell whether progress toward the goal was actually being achieved or if there was just a sense of activity.

Sixth, there must be a model for the successful completion of each task. Without a model, those auditing the change will have nothing to compare it to, and those attempting the change will have nothing to imitate. The model might be some experiment or demonstration project in the institution or in a neighboring institution. If no model exists, it would be wise to construct a pilot and make sure it is workable before proceeding. The "model" might be found in the experience of outside consultants or even in a book, but there must be something. If performance is poor, then perhaps a better model is needed.

Seventh, as performance begins, it must be shaped. Progress toward the goal must be strengthened, and all other activity must receive no encouragement. This feedback must be immediate, and it must be structured. People must know whether what they are doing meets expectations. It must be objective—not allowing one person to feel encouraged and another person doing the same thing to feel discouraged. It must be delivered systematically: It should not depend on "grapevines" to get the word around about how things are going. It must occur quite often in the beginning and occur immediately after performance—there should not be delays until monthly meetings or semi-annual reviews of staff performance. Other things in the institutional environment which would reward non-performance or which would counter the effect of rewarding successful performance must be eliminated.

Eighth, there must be reliable reporting so that feedback can occur. By working on specific tasks and attempting to approach an objective model, subjective and judgmental reporting should be avoided. Reporting should focus on evaluations of performance (was the task done) rather than opinions about attitudes (he likes his job; others like him). The latter is important but cannot have priority.

Ninth, decisions must be based on performance. Not only must attention be directed toward whether a performance occurred, but decisions about what the performance indicates must follow. *If an approach is working it should be continued; if it is not working it should be discontinued.*

Tenth, specific results must be communicated to outside parties in objective, intelligible terms. This communication is vital to the concepts of compliance and effectiveness because information in the hands of a third party can be a needed lever. Without it, the institution can simply claim to be effective and in compliance; with it, programs can be changed, funds can be cut, and persons can be fired or sued for violating the law. The communication should be in a usable form, not in the form of aggregate pictures so often presented to legislatures and other public bodies today.

Contracting for Performance: Setting the Goal

The previous chapter discussed contracting out for some specific services to clients. Rule six above suggests the need for a model to teach the desired behavior. If an institution does not have a working model, then it should consider contracting out for a demonstration project.[1] One advantage is that the contract could require the demonstration to occur under actual institutional conditions.[2] All too often, demonstrations occur under very special conditions, with federal and state laws waived during the experiment, with special funds, with volunteers among the staff, and so forth. If the demonstration is conducted under real conditions, with real staff, one can feel surer that a successful approach will indeed be effective over the long run.

A second advantage is that the contract can be drafted so that payment occurs only upon performance. This kind of procurement is practiced by many government agencies (although they often settle for increased costs and decreased performance) and has been considered in the social service area.[3] Some defendants in recent decisions requiring more effective services have argued that they could not afford the cost of doing better. They might "performance contract" the provision of services until they reach the effectiveness level required to be in compliance and can determine the actual cost. The experience in some cases has been that increased performance can actually occur with decreased costs.[4]

And with a "performance contract" demonstration, courts and legislatures can make more informed judgments about what is really possible in a professional sense and what is required to make it work. Payment on the basis of performance allows professionals to demonstrate the effectiveness of new techniques without costing the institution a lot of money.

The best reason for a performance contract in the field of behavior change is that all client rights can be assured of protection as a new technique is employed. If the new technique is simply grafted onto the ongoing institution, with all its idiosyncratic behavior, there is potential for abuse. But if it is demonstrated more carefully then it can be altered as needed. The steps in developing a performance-based contract—whether it brings in outside behavior change specialists or uses in-house resources—can assure that all essential legal questions are raised and kept in focus.

Auditing Behavior Change:
Evaluating Progress Toward the Goal

The degree to which our public institutions now concern themselves with individual behavior change means that substantial effort should be expended to monitor that effort. Currently available tools are really ineffective in evaluating compliance and effectiveness.

In 1967, Congress created a new bilingual education program.[5] Because of dissatisfaction with the reports on results of previous legislation which the Office of Education furnished each year, the Congress wanted to create a new tool of evaluation. Since the financial scandals of the 1920's, states had been requiring that schools audit their financial records and account for every cent, showing that it was being spent according to law. But what of the *worth* of those expenditures? The 1967 amendments required an audit of what was accomplished educationally and whether that was in furtherance of the law.

The Independent Educational Accomplishment Audit has had a spotty history, largely because auditors were chosen too casually by some school districts, with no uniform standards for performance. Some local districts put pressure on the auditors: If they did not produce a favorable report, they could not expect to obtain further contracts in that district. And some local districts simply refused to forward the reports.[6] As a result of the perserverance of a few highly professional educational auditors and staff within the Office of Education, a good concept has been kept alive and much could be learned from it. Independent Behavior Change Audits might be required as part of legislation dealing with social services, especially where that legislation already calls for research, demonstration, and evaluation. Audits could also be ordered by a court to determine if proper compliance is occurring.

Audits which produce comparable information about all behavior change strategies currently being used in an institution offer the best hope for finding out what is the best possible care for our citizens and how we can produce it. To suggest how thorough an audit might be, Figure 1 (pp. 104-5) indicates the stages necessary in preparing a program from admission to release.[7] Although it would have to be adapted to a specific institution, its use would force that institution to confront the questions of whether it offers some productive change, whether it has goals, whether the institutional environment supports progress toward those goals, whether an individual treatment program has been developed, and whether it is working. When this audit instrument was used in one institution, the new staff director kept asking, "Is that really what we are doing?" That question should be faced by all public services which attempt behavior change.

The newly emerging rights to education and treatment have not yet been converted into rights to *effective* education or treatment—but the trend is clear. The court in *PARC* said the child must be in school and the school must do something with him. They did not set any effectiveness criteria, but the next level of complaint in a *PARC* situation is that what the school is doing is not effective. In another case[8] the Department of Justice is suing on the grounds that the institution must bring about some change—not only that there must be treatment, but that the treatment must produce change. As the courts head into the area of effectiveness there will be even more reason for programs to audit behavior change.

CHAPTER 8 REVIEW QUESTIONS

1. Does your institution have behaviorally specific goals, written down in objective language?

2. Does the institution have sequenced tasks leading to the accomplishment of its goals?

3. Are there working models which illustrate the successful completion of tasks?

4. Is there accurate feedback on institutional performance,

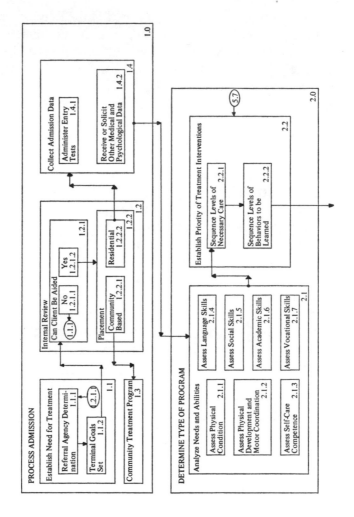

Figure 1
Treatment Model
from Admission
to Release

104

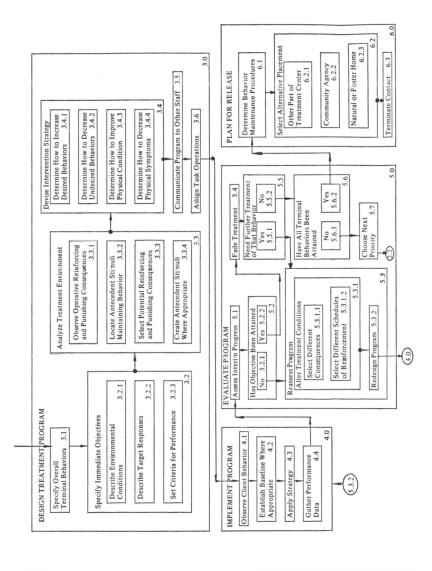

communicated both inside the institution and to the general public?

5. Is successful performance always rewarded more than non-performance?

6. Are approaches that do not work discarded?

7. Could your approach be attempted through a special performance-based contract which could better contrast your results with the institution's regular performance?

8. Does your institution have a system of auditing the way all facets of the institution affect behavior, whether it is a designated "behavior modification" project or just the traditional rewards and punishments structured into any institution?

9

Supervision and Control

SUMMARY[1]

Staff in many institutions do not seem to be under anyone's control. Too little attention is paid to the creation of positions, recruitment and selection of staff, pre-service and in-service training, and evaluation of staff performance and advancement and other rewards; supervisory staff may be liable for failure to really supervise or for failing to find out when something is going wrong and correcting it. Chapter 9 identifies common weaknesses in institutions' systems of staff training and supervision and describes remedial procedures.

THE NEED FOR SUPERVISION AND CONTROL OF STAFF

A person observing programs in today's public institutions is often compelled to ask the question "Is anyone in charge?" These public bodies are mandated by law to carry out very important behavior change functions but there seems to be little coordinated action toward any goal. A specialist in human behavior ought to be able to understand this, because there are layers of institutional behavior-shaping forces at work controlling the staff. But that often means that those "in charge" are not in control.

When a behavior change specialist introduces a program into an institution he must remain in charge. That often entails designing a program to deal with the staff in addition to the program directed at the clients.

The court in *Morales* found treatment of the staff extremely important. In fact, it suggested that placing a program in the hands of poorly trained staff violated constitutional requirements. It cited five problems in particular. The first problem is having insufficient staff to actually deal with the problem, so that there is in reality no program, and things might actually get worse. Second, staff members must be properly screened to assure they are not psychologically unfit for the job they must perform. Third, staff members cannot be allowed to make decisions beyond their level of competence. Some staff in the *Morales* case decided to segregate several youths away from the general population. They were not qualified to make such a determination and thus violated the youths' right to treatment. Fourth, training cannot be insufficient preparation for the job. And fifth, there must be follow-up on training in the form of on-the-job supervision. As the *Morales* court stated ". . . careful training of all staff, especially those who have the most regular and intimate contact with [the clients] is a paramount necessity. In-service training . . . is indispensable. This should include training in the techniques of handling [a client] and understanding his . . . behavior. Such training should also lead to the staff's comprehension of the effect of their demeanor and actions on the [clients] and to their analyzing the behavioral effect on themselves of the [clients'] actions."

Current training often falls far short of these requirements, and this has strong impact on the level of functioning of the staff. The professional who wants to meet the responsibility of being in charge of a program must recognize the problem.

PROCEDURES FOR DEVELOPING
AN EFFECTIVE STAFF

You cannot develop a program in a controlled experimental setting and then simply drop it into an ongoing institution and expect that it will run well. If prison guards have been intent upon breaking the spirit of prisoners, they can hardly be expected to take a behavior change technology and decide to use it humanely. If mental institution staff have been providing perpetual custodial care, they cannot be expected to understand or use a behavior change strategy—it does not fit their concept of the job. You must observe the staff to determine how and why they function before a new behavior change strategy is introduced.

Job Creation

Staffing procedures begin with job creation—the institution or even the state legislature creates a slot, with certain duties, pay, and so forth. It may bear no resemblance to what the behavior change specialist wants the person holding that job to do, but job creation will determine the raw material upon which he must depend. That position may turn out to be absolutely crucial to an effective program. The existing staff positions must be used—they cannot be supplanted just for one program; they cannot be worked around. So those concerned with how institutions influence behavior must start with how staff positions are created. This is not to say that good job creation will yield positive results, but it is to say that sloppy job creation will produce an unpredictable staff, and it will be harder to meet the legal responsibility to remain in charge.

Recruitment

The next step in staffing is recruitment. Who is attracted to this job slot? Suppose it is a low-paying, low prestige slot working with mentally retarded children. Recruitment could probably come from young people with a few years of college behind them and a desire to work, to do something useful and very rewarding, and to find out if this might be a career choice before they go back to finish their education. If that is the recruit, then he will likely be predisposed to change behavior through verbal interactions and will be impatient to see results. If the program is one of slow behavior change using simple rewards for simple tasks, then that type of staff person will not react well to training. If he finds it demeaning to work for several months on self-dressing behavior, rather than trying for some "human-to-human" interaction with a severely retarded child, and if he does not like to keep charts and graphs, then even a carefully designed program will simply not be carried out. And the legal responsibility for supervisory control will not be met.

Selection

Once a job is created and various recruits are available, the next crucial step is selection. Not surprisingly, many institutions use a purely subjective interview. If we know that a person will have to perform certain tasks at a certain level of ability, then the selection interview should use a technique which can objectively assess the interviewee's skill. The easiest process would be some task simulation, and it would serve a double purpose: The institution could determine whether the person fits the job; and the person will get an honest demonstration of what it is that he is to do if he takes the job. The kind of overqualified hiring that leads to increased cost of services, unrealistic expectations and thus job dissatisfaction, and eventually to high turnover rates (itself a cause of increasing cost of services) might be lessened by adequate selection procedures. Most important for our purposes, if the institution is to engage in a certain behavior change strategy, then selection could be relevant to whether the person will work effectively in the institution.

A critic might ask whether I am suggesting that institutions with unconventional plans for behavior modification should select spineless recruits who will not question authority and who will carry out any directions. Of course not—the point is that public institutions owe to their clients and to society in general the care to select persons who can carry out the institution's programs and not simply go off on their own, becoming totally unaccountable, fashioning their own approaches, becoming ineffective or possibly harmful. *Our institutions seem filled with persons who were hired having no idea what they were to do and, upon being told what their job was, decided to do something else instead.*

Training

Training is where the problems of poor job creation, poor recruitment and poor selection come together The expectation of most behavior change programs with which I am familiar is that, through training, the staff will learn what they need and will change. That training, however, often comes too late, for there are really several stages to staff training: orientation, pre-service, unplanned in-service, and planned in-service.

Orientation. Orientation usually occurs in an informal way with bits and pieces of shared information. If a new staff member learns that his level of performance cannot really be evaluated and that he is expected to report to no one in particular, then his perspective will be shaped a certain way. However, if he learns that his tasks are quite observable, that reporting and evaluation is systematic, and that action follows upon evaluation, he will respond in a much more accountable way.

Pre-service training. Before actually carrying out tasks with regard to the resident population, the new staff member will probably receive some formal pre-service training. This is usually academic rather than task-related. I have observed many staff persons who received training in structured learning approaches in pre-service classes, who scored high on an academic test, and who then entered their daily work area and found no way to actually apply their new academic knowledge, although they continue to discuss it in an academic context with their fellow staff members at such a high rate that an observer would assume a behavior change program was fully underway.

Unplanned in-service training. Unplanned in-service training is the stage where an institution permanently shapes the behavior of the staff member. He learns what is really wanted of him, what really impresses his supervisors, what he will be held accountable for, and what will go unevaluated. He may learn that written evaluation reports are filed with no response but unrecorded personal chats make the institution run. Once that lesson is learned, if the behavior change program is dependent upon written evaluations, effective control will be impossible.

Planned in-service training. Planned in-service training is probably where most programs of behavior change are attempted. But look at the obstacles: A job has been created; a certain type of individual has been recruited; a selection has been made without any explanation of what the person is getting into; the person learns through orientation and unplanned in-service training what he is really supposed to be doing; and he has learned from academic pre-service training to be leery of new strategies. For planned in-service training to be successful, one must first observe the institution at work to determine what the unplanned rewards and punishments really are. Then the planned training must take those into account. If it does not, it will not produce predictable behavior change in the staff. *A training program that will unleash some behavior change strategy with no predictable result, because of lack of attention to administrative control over the staff, will not only fail but should not be allowed in a public institution in the first place.*

Evaluation and Advancement

The next major administrative step is evaluation. The key is whether the staff evaluation is related to observable and measurable tasks. Most evaluation instruments are like the selection interview instruments: Does he work well with others? Is he liked by the staff? Does he seem to want to make a career of his job? Those are useful questions which a bureaucracy understandably ponders, but a more relevant question to ask is does he do his job. That is usually not asked because it would force the institution to define what the job is. If the job is broken down into specific tasks and each task is measured objectively, then evaluation can occur. Otherwise there is no evaluation, only perpetuation.

If evaluation is unrelated to the training program, then two common phenomena will occur: A staff member's behavior will be totally unchanged by training but he will receive high evaluation, or a staff member will perform very well in the new program but will be evaluated just the same. A related problem is lack of continuity between levels of evaluation. The behavior change program may seem successful at one level, but if federal, state, or local evaluators are using different criteria that success may be judged a failure.

The final step in staffing procedures is rewarding a successful employee through advancement or some other incentive. Many incentives in public institutions (salary, rates of increase, time off, working hours, working conditions) are set by legislatures, contract negotiations, scarcity of funds, or are otherwise rigid. They cannot be made contingent upon specific performance in order to motivate a change in staff behavior. However, other incentives can be created, such as new responsibilities or publishing monographs describing successful staff work with clients.

The overwhelming legal significance of staffing procedures is that if no attention is given to them then no one will be in control of the way these institutions change the behavior of their clients. Legislatures will not know what is being done, and there is no way of assuring that compliance with judicial decrees is occurring. And, needless to say, no new program of behavior change can be assured of any chance of succeeding. Once a specific abuse occurs, a lawsuit might stop it in that one instance but worse abuses might go undetected, and no affirmative plan to correct the abuses can be entered into with confidence. For these reasons, both behavior change programs and their critics stand to gain by making staff actions visible and accountable. Figure 2 (pp. 114-5) provides a guide which has proven useful in analyzing staff procedures and institutional responsibility.

INDIVIDUAL RESPONSIBILITY
The question of individual responsibility in regard to a client often arises. *Donaldson,* a case in which a jury assessed money damages against the individual in charge of the treatment program, has not escaped the attention of the profession. That case turned on the total failure to provide any treatment. Suits under the United States Code, Title 42, section 1983, proceed under a claim of violation of constitutional rights by a person acting under color of state

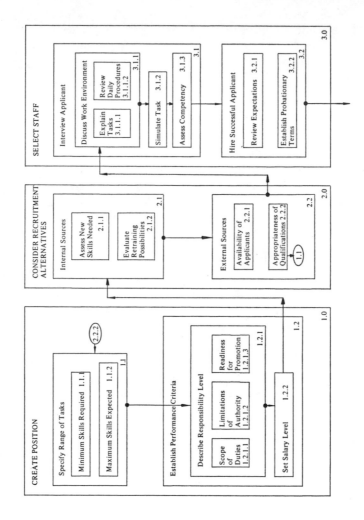

Figure 2
Staffing Procedures

114

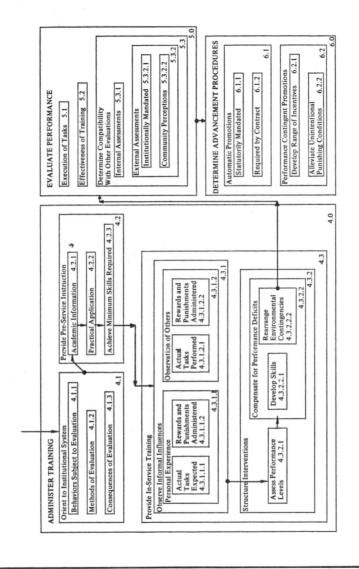

authority. A professional working for, or under contract to, a public institution would most likely be in that category, but courts have held professionals immune from virtually everything but absolute neglect. If you are operating under a stated policy, performing a governmental function, and have a good faith belief that what you are doing is constitutionally permissible, then you might escape legal liability for injury to a client.

However, there are three types of situations which make the professional more likely to lose a legal challenge. The first involves failing to distinguish between behavior change techniques that can be practiced by a non-physician and those more properly conducted by a psychiatrist. Most behavior change practitioners are psychologists, counselors, sociologists, or social workers. When working in a public institution their duties may overlap with those of licensed physicians including psychiatrists. The lines of authority must be clearly delineated in that case. Where a behavior change program might succeed without medication, but the physician has prescribed medication, any differences must be settled between professionals. Medication should not be terminated or even lessened by a non-physician. An obvious problem arises with the widespread abuse of medication that exists in many institutions. Without an actual treatment plan, and even without specific authorization, a new inmate is likely to be automatically drugged. A non-physician could well oppose this indiscriminate drug use and might convince nurses or other aides dispensing drugs to stop.[2] But it might raise real questions of liability, for the non-physician might be seen as leaving his privileged function and treading into an area where he does not belong.

A second area of potential liability concerns staff. As detailed above, there are many problems just in dealing with regular employees. But researchers and teachers often bring students along. Similarly, behavior change practitioners often recognize that a custodial aide who is very low on the organizational chart may, because of regular and intimate contact with the client, be the most important behavior change agent. So the professional may give larger duties to that person. The doctrine of *respondeat superior* requires the master to answer for the acts of his aide. Although there are many limitations on this doctrine, it might raise the question of how far you can allow a student or a pseudo-professional aide to go. In one infamous case in Florida,[3] aides with very little training were allowed to virtually run a program with adolescent retarded boys and violated many of their rights. The test will probably be the adequacy of supervision. If you can be present and personally supervise or direct the acts of a student or an aide, then the problem of liability is greatly lessened.

The third area is not yet well defined by the law but it is a logical corollary of the above discussion, and that is an affirmative duty to find out when something is going wrong and to stop it. This is a large responsibility, for so much can go wrong, but we cannot allow those in charge of public programs to simply say, "I didn't know it wasn't working." *The New York State Association for Retarded Children* case well established the notion that a person commits a wrong if he simply stands by and lets things get worse. So there is a duty to find out and to correct.[4] The behavior change specialist, especially if he applies an institutional behavior model such as in the previous chapter, a staff supervision model such as in Figure 2, and a program review model such as in Figure 1, could certainly know enough about what was happening to feel that he was escaping liability by adequately discharging this duty.

CHAPTER 9 REVIEW CHECKLIST

1. Do you have sufficient staff to actually meet your individual treatment goals?

2. Do staff positions exist appropriate to the tasks needed to be performed for treatment?

3. Are staff selected on the basis of demonstrated fitness

for tasks they will be expected to perform?

4. Does your program have pre-service and continuing in-service training?

5. Is staff performance evaluated in relation to measurable client progress?

6. Are staff who perform well rewarded more than other staff?

7. Do the supervisors adequately supervise staff, particularly aides or students?

8. Are supervisors and staff told of developments in the law so that they can reasonably know the rights of those in their care?

9. Does the institution have some system by which it would be able to find out if a client's rights were being violated in order to correct the problem?

10

Records

SUMMARY

Records should be related solely to the overt behaviors to be changed, and data obtained from secondary sources or from tests may be susceptible to challenge. Those in charge of records should take care that the client is not stigmatized and that information is not too easily available to others. Behavior change practitioners themselves may become the subject of controversy as records of decision-making about client treatment are opened to public scrutiny.

PRIVACY

Since the essence of many behavior change programs is objective data, record keeping becomes almost an art form. But it is also one of the most hotly contested areas because of the potential invasion of privacy.

What is the subject of the record keeping? If it is not related to anything in particular but is a fishing expedition to build data for a research project, then it may well represent an unwarranted invasion of privacy. For example you might follow the behavior of a group of students, then isolate those who run afoul of the law and see if any earlier behaviors might be correlated[1] —potentially interesting, but hardly permissible without consent.

THE NATURE OF THE DATA:
HOW IS IT OBTAINED?

Assuming there is a more legitimate, defined, and manageable scope to the government's interest in obtaining data, the question of how the data is to be obtained arises. Behavior programs often begin with a period of observation.

In order to get a true baseline, the practitioner would want to observe a person without his knowledge so that he would not knowingly alter his behavior. There may be questions of others' privacy as well if the observation occurs in a community environment. If the observation is not done directly by the researcher and he instead employs others to report on the subject, that may create worse problems (as well as raising serious research problems of reliability and bias). One solution might be to teach self-reporting skills to the potential client, or to get him to volunteer someone in his environment to observe, record, and report data.

It is likely there will be much data obtained through secondary sources rather than through direct observation. If testing is used, then legal restraints on consent (see Chapter 3) and problems of bias of certain tests (see Chapter 2) must be faced. Anyone conducting tests today can expect challenges to the right to test, to the interpretation of results, and to the decisions based on those interpretations.

Consequently, some persons do not conduct their own tests but instead rely on others. Again the question is how that data is obtained. It might involve illegal access. A behavior change specialist might gain access to records that he is not legally entitled to. In one project dealing with juveniles, police freely gave the behavior research team copies of records which state law required to be kept confidential. The behavior research team never breached their trust (they were apparently more careful with the records than were the police) but the access was illegal, and the project was nearly terminated. In another project the school board allowed student records to be examined by a private education firm selecting students for a special program. This access, although useful, was of questionable legality. When you have an opportunity to review records you must first determine that your access is lawful.

A practitioner may also be tempted to compile records, and thus form the decisions about behavior change programs, on the basis of profiles developed by others. Many government programs are now beginning to share so much data that with information from social welfare records, data from school, observations from public housing, and so forth, a personality profile could be easily developed. Such an accumulation of data would be hopelessly suspect as a base upon which to make decisions about a potential client.

There must be limits on the scope of the record keeping (related directly to the institution's sole business—e.g. academic performance) and there must be standards by which to test the validity (objectivity and verifiability) of items collected. There must be opportunities to review the file periodically and then contest certain items by having them either removed or explained through amplification, or by providing additional information. For example, if a psychological test shows a child has a low IQ, there should be an opportunity to conduct further tests and add that conflicting or confirming data to the file. Ideally, any truly inaccurate data would be deleted, but at the very least there should be rebuttal information on the record. The subject of the file should also be informed any time a decision is to be based on the information in the file.

Behavior change programs based on the structured learning approach do not seem too troubled by this problem because of their concentration on current, actual, overt, observable behavior. And their record keeping is in the form of highly visible data. But there are still several potential problems.

THE NATURE OF THE FILE

Practitioners of any behavior change strategy must face the problem of stigmatizing the client.[2] A person who is the recipient of psychological services may encounter prejudicial attitudes in many people, and his "past" might also adversely affect later educational or employment opportunities. For instance, in at least one school project dealing with "normal" children, but funded by the National Institute of Mental Health's Center for Studies of Crime and Delinquency, some parents feared that their children would become part of the permanent record of a study of pre-delinquents, and they had to consider asking that their children be removed from the project.

This issue can also be raised with respect to the cumulative records maintained in many schools. An amendment to the most recent federal Elementary and Secondary Education Act[3] provides new rights to parents in regard to seeing these school records, and this accountability through visibility should cure many faults. The cumulative file should no longer be a garbage pail into which any subjective and unverified comment about attitudes, home environment, and so forth can be dumped.

Another problem is the secondary use of data. If you want to publish research, then you should report data in a way that no individual can be identified. It is best to secure consent to publish results even though they will be disguised. Although you may be able to control your own secondary use of data, you must be careful that others do not have access. Some funding agency guideline may require your data to be merged into a bottomless computerized data-bank network, so that the subject of your pre-delinquent study shows up in law enforcement agency records across the country.

A final problem involves purging files. After a certain period of time after which you have no further contact with an individual, it seems logical that all individual records should be destroyed. This may well be required of all public research and treatment programs in the future, and those who choose to store records on computers will face a great difficulty because other data might be destroyed as well. There are a few behavior change specialists who use data in longitudinal studies and who run so many analyses that computers are necessary. In those cases, using coded data and making sure that the computerized data is not merged into larger data-banks would seem to assure sufficient client privacy and also protect the researcher from facing a difficult challenge from a single former client.

RECORDS OF ADMINISTRATIVE DECISIONS
In addition to maintaining records on clients involved in

research and treatment, behavior change specialists are also involved with their institutions in ways that produce a different kind of record. These have previously been internal decision-making matters and have not been publicly disclosed. But recently enacted Open Records Acts in some states contemplate opening these to public scrutiny. For example, decisions by hospital authorities dealing with administration and affecting individual cases might become available. This will take years to be worked out in terms of guidelines and further legislative clarification but the trend is excellent. It will expose institutions that lack adequate recording of individual treatment programs.[4] By making the procedure of decision-making visible, it should make the substance upon which decisions are made much more tangible.[5] That should also favor a structured learning approach.

At the federal level, the Freedom of Information Act[6] is forcing light into previously closed chambers.[7] Parole board decisions which were absolutely arbitrary and seemingly capricious—were based on no solid information, and did not have to be explained to anyone—are now subject to scrutiny and contest. Parole boards and their decisions are considered covered under the Freedom of Information Act and written decisions will now be made public.[8] In institutions using indeterminate sentencing the same logic should apply. The precise standard by which a person is judged ready for release must be written down, and all the evidence considered for and against the judgment must be available to impartial scrutiny. The pressure for more behaviorally specific and accountable decision-making should increase; questioning the nature of data and documentation is a crucial aspect of this trend.

CHAPTER 10 REVIEW CHECKLIST

1. Does your institution have written rules which govern record keeping?

2. Are your records directly related to overt behavior which justifies a behavior change program?

3. Is information obtained without violating the privacy of the potential client?

4. Are records which are relied upon objective and verifiable, or are they made up of subjective bits of information which seem significant only because of cumulative weight?

5. Are files reviewed periodically to remove extraneous items?

6. Are subjects of record keeping allowed access to their files?

7. Does the subject have an opportunity to challenge items in his record and either have them removed or insert rebuttal information?

8. Do you maintain files in such a way that if you had to purge someone's record you could do so? Could you also remove the record from the file of anyone to whom you allowed access?

9. Are subjects of record keeping informed whenever a decision is made on the basis of their file?

10. Must the subject give consent before anyone else may see the records? If not, do you at least inform the subject whenever his record is made available to someone else?

11. When your institution makes a determination about an individual do you have a written record of that decision-making process and the data on which the decision was based?

11

Remedies

SUMMARY

If a behavior change client initiates legal action he might ask for release from a program; he might try to stop the program completely for a variety of constitutional reasons; or he might seek money damages against the institution or individual supervisors. The behavior therapy profession itself might pursue private remedies in the form of self-regulation in order to prevent programs from reaching an abusive stage, and public remedies by the legislative or judicial branches will probably take the form of regulating experiments and aversive techniques more closely. The effectiveness of judicial remedies may well depend on a court's willingness to continue jurisdiction of a case and see that compliance occurs. If attempts to remedy the growing problems in the behavior modification field are specific in regard to the approaches they seek to curb, then truly abusive practices can be singled out and client rights protected without blocking other therapeutic efforts.

LEGAL REMEDIES

This book has detailed many ways that behavior change projects can go wrong from a legal point of view. When problems do arise there are a variety of possible remedies, some involving legal action brought on behalf of subjects of behavior change efforts.

One remedy being resorted to today is a suit for release from the institution on the grounds that, since there is a constitutional right to treatment, and since the individual claims there is no treatment offered, due process requires release. Where a behavior change project is the only treatment being offered and it is the type of group-tier-point system described in *Morales,* then a court might find it in effect "no treatment" and demand release. It is more likely, however, that a court would simply require that other types of treatment be tried.

The complaint about "behavior modification" is seldom that too little action is occurring but rather that what is occurring is too extreme: It is more likely that the suit would be to stop treatment by claiming that it violated constitutional rights. Placing a person in isolation because of something he said, with no opportunity to practice his religion or to associate with others, may violate the First Amendment.[1] If the program leads to a severe change in status or if personal property is taken away and used as a reward to be earned, it may violate the Fifth Amendment.[2] If the individual is deprived of social contact and thus effectively barred from access to an attorney, the Sixth Amendment may be violated.[3] If mental or physical cruelty is involved in the program, particularly through sensory deprivation, seclusion, substandard living conditions, or aversive conditioning, it may violate the Eighth Amendment.[4] If inmates are forced to do meaningless and repetitive chores purely to provide cheap labor for the institution, then the Thirteenth Amendment may be violated.[5] And if state programs cause one class of people, particularly one race, to be treated substantially differently than others, or provide disciplinary sanctions without due process, the Fourteenth Amendment may be violated.[6]

The complainant might ask for an injunction to stop the treatment immediately, or he might ask for damages against the institution or even from a specific person in charge. In addition to constitutional violations, specific complaints might include battery (unauthorized touching), false imprisonment (unauthorized restraint), lack of proper treatment, or psychiatric torts such as invasion of privacy or intentional infliction of emotional distress.

Such lawsuits are necessary where a specific wrong occurs, and they may solve the problem as far as the specific individual is concerned, but they may not create a better program or a better opportunity for treatment for others.

PRIVATE REMEDIES:
PROFESSIONAL SELF-REGULATION

The most immediate "remedy" is the private one that could come from professional self-regulation. This is a highly delicate area, and I am hesitant to intrude except to point out certain opportunities. Some method of self-regulation would inevitably prevent many occurrences which might lead to individual lawsuits or even more sweeping legislative safeguards. Since behavior change agents come from a variety of professions, existing professional codes and sanctions might not suffice. Several professionals have pointed out the many problems with licensing or certification,[7] but the old cliche is true—if the profession does not regulate its activity then someone else will.

One function of regulation would be to establish some professional standards so that unqualified persons would be screened out. When problems arose, the body could carry out a disciplinary function and perhaps even engage in retraining. Such a body could provide communication about potentially problem-causing programs and suggest preventive measures. For new techniques or experimental applications, there could be a review panel of peers to provide an early warning on problems. With the *Wyatt* decision many public institutions will be setting up Human Rights Committees, and it would be productive for professional review panels to be in liaison with them.

When objections are raised to projects there seem to be only two alternatives: continuation or termination. But with a recognized professional group it might be possible to negotiate differences, curing the defect before it becomes fatal, and thus allowing the program to continue.

PUBLIC REMEDIES: PUBLIC REGULATION

Executive Remedies

Aside from this area of private remedy, much could be

done publicly by all branches of government. The quickest help could come from the executive branches with regulations that place objective, certifiable standards on training. Allotted money should be spent only in relation to performance: performance of staff in accomplishing specified levels of skill and performance of clients in meeting specific program goals. In the field of education there is current discussion of "competency-based instruction" in which specific skills are detailed and trainees continue only if they progress. If the executive branches of whatever level of government were held accountable for training effective staff, many problems in institutions would be remedied.

A second executive remedy would be to apply provisions of the Administrative Procedures Act[8] to institutions involved in behavior change. Basically, this would require written rules about the substance of decisions, the process by which decisions are going to be made, and open hearings to make these decisions. Records of hearings would be available, and a better informed public could press for programs to be run in accordance with stated objectives. Where the hearing record showed the decision did not follow rules or was not justified by the record, the decision could be overturned.

Legislative Remedies

Whether the legislative body concerned is the federal Congress or a local City Council, the need is for objectively stated standards dealing with concepts of accountability, effectiveness, and adequacy. The legislation needs to provide incentives for compliance and penalties for noncompliance. In one experiment several years ago in California, schools were required to meet certain minimum objectives. Those that did got their previous year's budget plus a percentage increase. Those that did not got a reduction. The traditional rule for funding is that more money goes to the agency with the worst results. This *seems* logical: They must need the money. But in this experiment, where there was no incentive for just doing the same old job, results actually improved. Unfortunately almost no legislation contains an incentive for effective compliance or a penalty for conducting a half-hearted or demonstrably ineffective effort.

Experimentation. Legislative bodies must also seek to remedy abuses in behavior change by more specific regulation of seven areas. First is the area of experimentation. Experiments must have some scientific merit; they must not be conducted just to give graduate students something to do. There must be an acceptable level of risk which is lower than the benefits that will accrue to the subject, the profession's knowledge, and the public in general. There must be consent from the subject. There must be mechanisms for review of program plans and program progress which produce objective public data demonstrating the results of the approach. And safeguards must be built in to protect individual privacy and confidentiality of information while at the same time providing objective information to the public.

Bio-behavioral instrumentation. Second, bio-behavioral instrumentation that would be implanted in the brain must be controlled by legislatures. Waivers can always be granted for legitimate experiments, and if carefully controlled research ever demonstrates any benefits of electrical stimulation of the brain or other such approaches, then specific legislation might permit it. But what we have now is a permissive vacuum in which experimenters and nonaccountable public agencies could move too quickly. We need a buffer zone of prohibitive legislation which would place the burden of proof on the experimenter.

Psychosurgery. Similarly, psychosurgery should be more specifically regulated. Legislatures must create citizen panels to review every single request for surgically entering a person's brain to alter his behavior. Legislatures must require specific follow-up studies to determine effectiveness. There should be severe criminal penalties for failure to comply with the law. The mystique of the brain surgeon and his dramatic experiments must be overcome by objective data assessed by panels with lay representation.

Drugs. The use of drugs to alter behavior is radically increasing. When PTA meetings feature drug salesmen as speakers we know we need tighter regulation. Legislatures must require more data on drugs before they are sanctioned for use by state agents to affect behavior, more controls on the prescription and dispensing of drugs, and rigorous follow-up studies on effectiveness. Drugs which raise any questions about risks should be kept off the market; currently the burden of proof is upon the public to prove a drug harmful before it can be removed.

Electroconvulsive therapy. Fifth, the use of electricity in electroconvulsive therapy and aversive shock therapy should be specifically regulated. The number of times such therapy can be administered to a single individual over a specific period of time should particularly be determined. Conditions for proper consent and mechanisms for review should be legislatively mandated as should be follow-up studies on effectiveness.

Aversive therapy. The use of aversive therapy in public institutions should be severely limited. If the use of drugs can be controlled, if electric shock can be effectively regulated, and if basic rights are accorded to all institutional inmates so that deprivation of food, clothing, and so forth cannot be used, then aversive conditioning will practically be avoided. Legislative regulation of any aversive techniques should be very explicit so that its misuse becomes aversive to the practitioner.

Punishment. Seventh, legislatures have never come to grips with the many ways punishment is used in our society. Corporal punishment laws in school and child abuse laws applied to homes seem to regulate this area. But any professional knows that physical force and the threat of physical force are commonly employed methods of behavior change in most institutions.[9] They need regulation just as surely as do the more exotic techniques.

Judicial Remedies

Remedies in the judicial area are much harder to accomplish. A court must depend on whatever case reaches it and whatever issues are implicit in that case; thus sweeping remedies are unlikely. When remedies are established, they are often limited further by lack of follow-up or enforcement. Courts might better effect remedies by continuing jurisdiction over certain types of cases. The argument for not doing this is that courts get such poor data from agencies that it is too much work to see that a decision is being carried out and is having the desired impact. If courts required the production of data along the lines detailed in Chapter 8, they might strengthen remedies they have developed. Other alternatives would be for the court to set a specific future date to review progress in compliance with its order in the particular case, or to establish an independent panel to oversee whatever compliance it requires.

A final judicial remedy might lie in the area of a taxpayer suit to force effective use of funds. There are terrific obstacles to this: whether a specific taxpayer has standing to sue; what is the standard that the complainant argues is not being met; and whether the result will force the judiciary to adopt a basically legislative role by deciding how funds are to be spent. But analogous efforts have been made in education and other social service sectors may not be far behind.

LET'S BE SPECIFIC
Whether the remedy is a private one or is in the legislative, executive, or judicial area, the first step is to work with specific terms. Terms such as "behavior modification" and "aversive conditioning" are far too subjective to be of use. What is needed is behavioral specificity, to describe behavior modification and aversive conditioning by specifying the actual techniques and their impact. Labels can be highly misleading. Some "humanistic" sensitivity sessions can destroy vulnerable participants, and some "behavior modification" can be very humane. Without precisely defining the approach being restricted, all those working with similar clients or with similar techniques may be effectively hampered in their efforts. We cannot expect news media to take the extra space to differentiate between applications, but we must demand it from our government agencies if we are to

provide our citizens with the best care possible and protect them from the worst abuses imaginable.

CHAPTER 11 REVIEW CHECKLIST

1. Is the program offering so little treatment that clients should be released from it?

2. Does the program violate any client constitutional rights?

3. Have any staff inflicted any injury, either physical or psychological, that could have been avoided?

4. Could professions governing the staff regulate their conduct in a way that would curb any abuse now being seen?

5. Can the problem with the approach be solved through some administrative negotiation process rather than simply terminating the program?

6. Could abuses be brought to light and/or corrected if executive agencies responsible for programs required additional kinds of information?

7. Can specific abuses and needs for effective therapy be brought to the attention of legislative bodies in a way that positive legal regulation might occur?

8. Should some approaches simply be banned outright?

9. If a judicial decree is sought as a remedy, can the court be convinced to continue the jurisdiction of the case and force the production of information about compliance with the decree?

12

Conclusion

SUMMARY

Some powerful behavior modifying influences in our society such as advertising and politics are not covered in this book since we have limited ourselves to explicit programs of behavior change. There is a danger that overzealous practitioners of these behavior change programs may try to take the technology too far. For instance, the notion of licensing parenthood proceeds from a concern for the future of all children but may open a Pandora's box of government interference in private lives. Other proposals suggest that we institute macrosystems of behavior change on populations over which the government already holds the power to manipulate such rewards as welfare. Public outcry and backlash to such ill-advised proposals could jeopardize all behavior change programs in a wide range of state institutions.

THE NEED TO REGULATE
"BEHAVIOR MODIFICATION"

There are many forces in today's society seeking to modify our behavior which could not be the subject of this book. The enormous energy that goes into advertising and causes consumers to overspend billions of dollars is worthy of mention but the whole psycho-business world and the failure to regulate it are enough for another book.

Similarly, the use of psychological techniques in politics begs for further analysis. Using the television medium, some candidates have consciously tried to associate certain stimuli and condition audiences into permanent response patterns. The usual safeguard is the candidate's competition, which presumably sways the public back toward neutral. But what happens when there is no competition—when a President of the United States goes on all television networks at once? A few years ago the author of a book on brain research was interviewed on NBC-TV's "Today" show. He was asked which of all those techniques described in his book[1] —electrode implantation, surgery, and so forth—would a totalitarian force choose to control the behavior of the mass of Americans. The author replied quickly that nothing yet imagined had the power of a televised address by a President, complete with a bust of Lincoln and other props chosen for their psychological impact on the audience. Lawyers have certainly not yet determined ways to regulate such gross abuses any more than behavioral scientists have demonstrated how to countercondition a freshly brainwashed electorate.

Two of the largest behavior modifiers in our society—business and politics—are not treated here. Our concern has been the practice of explicit programs of behavior change. The frequently stated concern has been that techniques which hold great promise may win disfavor because of abuse by overzealous proponents or through misuse by government agents attempting large programs. Two examples which have been widely discussed and might be seriously proposed in the future are the concept of licensing parenthood and the notion of token economy systems for welfare recipients. Perhaps a fuller examination of them will illustrate the damage overenthusiastic behavior modifiers might do to themselves.

Licensing Parenthood

The seemingly logical extension of changing deficient behavior in already troubled individuals is the prevention of similar problems in others. Some behavior modifiers, after seeing so many children damaged by parents' actions, argue that proper education of parents in childrearing techniques would have prevented the injury. Parent education materials are among the largest selling behavior modification books, and the U.S. Office of Education is currently conducting a pilot "Education for Parenthood" program in secondary schools. But a few behavior modifiers are not content with voluntary education. They argue that education after parenthood is too late and that all parents will not undertake it anyway. Thus they propose a parenthood license;[2] before a person can conceive or adopt a child, he must be certified.

The first objection is that there is a right to have children, or at least there is no superior right inherent in the state which would support the concept of a license. Proponents of licensing argue that society collectively does have a superior right because we bear the burden of sociopathic actions and must pay the bills for institutional care. Further, they argue, they are not taking away the right to parenthood, they are merely taking it out of the range of chance and placing it under the management of a new contingency. This is the same argument invoked to manipulate rights in mental institutions and prisons, and courts are likely to deny its validity.

Assuming for the sake of argument that there could be such a license, what would comprise the test? Proponents confidently assume that the required skills would all be behavior modification techniques. Passing over the fact that even behavior modifiers do not agree on childrearing—some detest Time Out, others would allow aversive control, and so forth—it is likely that each state legislature would create its own test. Since behavior modification is somewhat new, somewhat innovative, and somewhat unproven, the list of required skills would probably lean heavily toward traditional techniques—what state legislator would vote for procedures significantly different from the way he was raised? At best, there would be a range from which to choose, but there would certainly not be unanimity on structured learning approaches (it is more likely that some states would expressly forbid them).

But assuming that there was a set of "parent" skills, how could their proper use be tested? Behaviorists, of all people, would be forced to admit that as environments change, people change. Assume that two twenty-year-olds pass their test, have a child, move to a congested part of New York City, learn new aggressive behaviors, become alcoholic, lose their jobs, and take out their frustration on their child. How could a license test prevent that?

The obvious answer is that it would not, but that a license, by definition, can be revoked. A dual spectre then arises: The child would become a ward of the state and would be raised in institutions; or the child would be held by the state until the parents somehow earned the child back. The youngster would be in and out of the home and the institution. In most urban areas the reality of foster home placement is such that the child would be detained in an institution, on a waiting list, until age eighteen. That would hardly produce the perfect children that are the justification for the behavior modifiers' enthusiasm.

One final objection is that unlicensed parents might still have children, thus defeating the system. Would they then "belong" to the state, to be raised in institutions? Some proponents of licensing have a final answer—compulsory birth control. Not willing to contemplate voluntary compliance they would implant chemical substances in the body to cause temporary sterilization. Having thus established the precedent of allowing the state to violate the individual's body, the next step would be easy—altering the chemicals to include behavior modifying drugs, or even adding an electrical component to monitor and modify behavior.

Thus there may be a logical continuum linking the most caring forms of behavioral intervention—helping children— and the most threatening applications of behavior control— instrumental control of adults. Licensing parenthood is one of the bridges between the two poles. If licensing proponents really press their case, they may provoke such public backlash that all forms of behavior therapy will be endangered.

Welfare Tokens
If licensing parenthood is an example of potential abuse by overzealous proponents, a proposed New York welfare experiment demonstrates the threat of a large government sponsored system. In the spring of 1971, the Department of Health, Education and Welfare proposed to three states (New York, California, and Illinois) that in their application for welfare funds they ask for an experimental waiver

under the Aid to Families with Dependent Children (AFDC) program.[3] Illinois turned the offer down, California delayed, but New York accepted the offer.[4] The proposal was to separate out several thousand families whose sole support was welfare, take away a substantial portion of their monthly income, and then have it earned back in small dollar amounts for performing specified behaviors. Thus a child could earn points redeemable in dollars by supplying to federal officers leads as to the whereabouts of an absent parent, and a mother could earn points by forcing her child to follow the teacher's instructions. If a teacher felt a child was uncooperative, a simple complaint could wipe out points—and thus hold up next month's groceries.[5]

The plan was still being finalized in secret when a suit by the National Welfare Rights Organization, under the Freedom of Information Act, forced it into the light of day where it quickly died. But as resentment over growing welfare rolls increases, the threat of re-enactment is there. Several behavior modifiers with whom I have discussed the plan have instinctively defended it. Two arguments are most usually advanced: that it is no harsher than the real world in which one has to do certain tasks in order to bring in a monthly check, and that this opportunity to change behavior should not be missed, since the state holds such a powerful reinforcer in its hands. The lessons of this book—determine if you have a right to act, determine if you can help, determine if you are establishing a precedent that will make future abuses more likely—are lost on one who can make such an argument.

Not all behaviorists feel that every lever of power should be used—many doubt their own skills and, more importantly, they doubt the wisdom of government institutions. Justice Learned Hand once wrote that the spirit of liberty is the spirit that is not too sure it is right. Behavior modification practitioners and administrators must reinforce a similar feeling of limitation in their work if they are to continue to offer services without destructive legal regulation.

137

Notes

CHAPTER ONE

1. See, for example: *Stroud v. Swope,* 187 F.2d. 850 (9th Cir. 1951) at 851: "[It] is not the function of the courts to superintend the treatment and discipline of prisoners in penitentiaries. . . ." See also: "Beyond the Ken of the Courts: A Critique of Judicial Refusal to Review the Complaints of Convicts." 72 Yale L.J. 506 (1963).

2. "He is for the time being the slave of the State." *Ruffin v. Commonwealth,* 62 Va. (21 Gratt.) 790, 796 (1871).

3. The Fifth Amendment to the Constitution provides, in part, "No person shall be . . . deprived of life, liberty, or property, without due process of law . . . ." The Fourteenth Amendment applies the same prohibition to the states: ". . . Nor shall any state deprive any person of life, liberty, or property, without due process of law. . . . "

4. *In Re Gault* (see the Annotated Table of Cases) requires that a juvenile receive notice of the charges against him, the right to counsel at a hearing in which he can confront accusers and cross-examine them, the right to refuse to testify, the right to a transcript of the hearing, and the right to appeal. *Pennsylvania Association of Retarded Children v. Commonwealth of Pennsylvania* (see the Annotated Table of Cases), hereafter referred to as *PARC,* provides that whenever a child is recommended for change in status, notice will inform the parents as to

the proposed action and available alternatives, the right to contest the action at a hearing, the right to counsel, the right to examine all records, the right to produce expert witnesses, the right to question any school official with evidence, and the right to an independent evaluation. Furthermore, the hearing officer shall not be an employee of the school district, and there is a right to a stenographic transcript of the hearing.

5. The Fourteenth Amendment to the Constitution states, in part, "No State shall . . . deny to any person within its jurisdiction the equal protection of the laws."

6. All cases mentioned by name in the text are cited in full in the Annotated Table of Cases.

7. For a full description of Donaldson's condition, see: B. J. Ennis, *Prisoners of Psychiatry* (New York: Harcourt Brace Jovanovich, 1972), pp. 83-98.

8. *United States of America v. Dr. Neil Solomon* et al., Civil Action No. N 74-181, complaint filed in the United States District Court for the District of Maryland, February 21, 1974.

9. No attempt is made here to summarize guidelines. They vary from state to state. Federal guidelines issue from several agencies and seem to be in a state of permanent revision. Several new entities, such as the legislatively created National Commission for the Protection of Human Subjects of Biomedical and Behavioral Research, will soon be issuing guidelines. The reader is simply cautioned to find the guidelines that pertain to his specific project.

10. See: M. Kozloff, *Reaching the Autistic Child: A Parent Training Program* (Champaign, Ill.: Research Press, 1973); B. Gray and B. Ryan, *A Language Program for the Nonlanguage Child* (Champaign, Ill.: Research Press, 1973); L. Kent, *Language Acquisition Program for the Retarded or Multiply Impaired* (Champaign, Ill.: Re-

search Press, 1975); R. G. Buddenhagen, *Establishing Vocal Verbalizations in Mute Mongoloid Children* (Champaign, Ill.: Research Press, 1971). Each of these books illustrates how people previously thought unreachable and unteachable have responded to careful behavior change strategies. This realization formed the sentiment in the *PARC* case that no child is beyond the hope of education and that the state is therefore obligated to try to help.

11. "There are today means of sustaining desirable behavior or modifying undesirable behavior which are precise, specific, predictable and effective. The methods have been demonstrated, supported by research findings, and are continuing to be developed. Materials . . . are available to make those methods available to educators who do not already have them." A. Reitman, J. Follman, and E. Ladd, *Corporal Punishment in the Public Schools: The Use of Force in Controlling Student Behavior* (New York: ACLU, 1972), p. 4. Cited as an example: N. Buckley, and H. Walker, *Modifying Classroom Behavior* (Champaign, Ill.: Research Press, 1970).

12. In Baltimore County Circuit Court, the Maryland State Department of Health sued for guardianship of an infant whose parents refused to allow surgery. The judge postponed the hearing indefinitely because the infant was too weak to undergo surgery anyway. In a New Hampshire case, custody was awarded to the state, but the infant died before surgery could be performed. The motive of the state seems to be that times are changing and that a severely physically and perhaps mentally handicapped individual can find a place in society. This does seem possible with the help of a supportive family with private resources. Ironically, the state's action on behalf of the child means that if it lives it will be a permanent ward of the state, and state institutions are not particularly effective in shaping normal behavior. Which is better for the child, life in a state hospital or

death, is a question of insoluble moral complexity. But the issue of who has a right, on behalf of the child, to make a decision about its future will be decided by courts and will affect any counselor dealing with children or wards of the state.

13. In Iowa, four children were taken away from their parents because a county probation officer felt things in the family were not as they should be. Suit has been brought to reunite the family and to overturn state laws which allow a family to be so arbitrarily dissolved.

14. American Civil Liberties Union, *Civil Liberties* (New York: Author, 1975), p. 7.

CHAPTER TWO

1. *Goss v. Lopez* (see the Annotated Table of Cases). The Supreme Court argued that a student charged with misconduct would receive a label which could damage his standing with his fellow students and his teachers, thus depriving him of an essential element of liberty. Such a classification is doubly important in educational institutions because it raises the due process prohibition against deprivation of property as well. The Court reasoned that any act which might interfere with the opportunity for higher education or employment would raise the issue of whether a property right was being affected.

2. Various standards have been used to determine when the state has a right to begin interfering with an individual's way of acting, but the most enduring is Mr. Justice Goldberg's suggestion in a concurring opinion that there must be a "compelling State interest" which is directly related to the accomplishment of a "permissible State policy." *Griswold v. Connecticut* (see the Annotated Table of Cases) at 497.

3. See: R. Light, "Abused and Neglected Children in America: A Study of Alternative Policies," *Harvard Educational Review*, November 1973, *43*(4), 556-98;

J. W. Polier, "Myths and Realities in the Search for Juvenile Justice: A Statement by the Honorable Justine Wise Polier," *Harvard Educational Review*, February 1974, *44*(1), 112-24.

4. Polier, note 3, suggests that some neglected children who find themselves under the scrutiny of the state are not simply neglected but may in fact be engaging in various criminal acts such as stealing or drug use. Where the act itself prompts intervention it would appear to be justified, but where there is no offending behavior on the part of the child, a behavior change program could be susceptible to attack.

5. "Doctor Pushes Crime Tests for Tots," *Washington Post,* April 14, 1970. "Dangers in Tendencies Tests," *Washington Star,* April 16, 1970. "Crime Tests for Tots Rejected by HEW," *Washington Post,* April 16, 1970. Reprinted in: *Federal Involvement in the Use of Behavior Modification Drugs on Grammar School Children of the Right to Privacy Inquiry.* Hearings before a subcommittee of the Committee on Government Operations, House of Representatives, Ninety-First Congress, Second Session, September 29, 1970. Pp. 141-3.

6. Social Security Act amendments provide for comprehensive preventive health care plans for children; Medicaid amendments mandate states to carry out "Early and Periodic Screening, Diagnoses, and Treatment" programs for children; and a pending amendment to an aid bill for education of the handicapped would provide bonuses for school systems that develop screening programs for three-year-olds.

7. C. Frankel, "Genetics: What Shall the Human Species Make of Itself?" *Washington Post,* April 21, 1974, p. B-1.

8. For an excellent discussion of types of observation and attendant problems, see: L. Keith Miller, *Principles of Everyday Behavior Analysis* (Monterey, Calif.: Brooks Cole, 1975).

9. This right was most eloquently stated by Mr. Justice Brandeis, dissenting in *Olmstead v. United States,* 277 U.S. 438 (1928) at 478: "The makers of our Constitution undertook to secure conditions favorable to the pursuit of happiness. . . . They sought to protect Americans in their beliefs, their thoughts, their emotions, and their sensations. They conferred, as against the Government, the right to be let alone—the most comprehensive of rights and the right most valued by civilized men."

10. Some prohibitions of IQ tests have been the result of a school's own initiative, but increasingly they are the result of a lawsuit, such as *Larry P. v. Riles*, 343 F.Supp. 1306 (N.D. Cal. 1972).

11. In the Washington, D.C. public schools a controversy arose over questionnaires which the Department of Health, Education and Welfare proposed to send to student participants in a special project. Questions probed home life and family relations, a common type of data gathered by schools and other agencies for many years. But the Washington, D.C. school board voted to prohibit the gathering of such data in the future.

12. "We now have what may be called a 6-hour retarded child—retarded from 9 to 3, five days a week, solely on the basis of an IQ score, without regard to his adaptive behavior, which may be exceptionally adaptive to the situation and community in which he lives." U.S. Commissioner of Education James E. Allen, Jr. speaking to a Conference on Problems of Education for Children in the Inner City, August 10, 1969, Airlie House, Warrenton, Virginia. In *Hobson v. Hansen*, 260 F.Supp. 401 (D.D.C. 1967), aff'd *sub nom. Smuck v. Hobson,* 408 F. 2d. 175 (D.C. Cir. 1969), the entire school system was run on four tracks to which students were assigned on the basis of IQ scores. Blacks were typically in the lower tracks and were slated for vocational courses while whites went on to college preparatory material. *Hobson* and many subsequent cases have declared that practice

illegal.

13. *Diana v. State Board of Education,* Civil Action No. 70-37 RFP (N.D. Cal. January 7, 1970 and June 18, 1973).

14. When simply the appearance of an attorney on the scene leads to release, one would certainly question the wisdom of the original commitment and the constitutionality of such easy admissions. In the case of the Northern Virginia gentleman, he felt that only a few hours of incarceration and the stigma from attendant publicity entitled him to damages from the police. If individuals who have used these laws so easily suddenly must pay a penalty for abuses of discretion, it might remedy the situation until the day such laws are declared unconstitutional.

15. In *In Re Staly,* 218 So.2d. 765 (D.Ct. App. Fla. 1969), two doctors testified that a "hippie" required treatment because he believed in free love and nonviolence and used hallucinogens. The court refused, stating: "The fact that he decided to lead the kind of life, entertain beliefs and engage in conduct which was offensive, repulsive and objectionable to others does not necessarily indicate mental incompetence, nor does it justify confining him to a mental institution."

16. M. Chesney-Lind, "The Sexualization of Female Crime," *Psychology Today,* July 1974, *8*(2), 93.

17. *Tinker v. Des Moines Independent Community School District,* 393 U.S. 503 (1969).

18. See: A. Neier, "Delinquency Predictions." In: A. Neier, *Dossier: The Secret Files They Keep on You* (New York: Stein and Day, 1975), pp. 36-47.

19. R.B. Stuart, *Trick or Treatment* (Champaign, Ill.: Research Press, 1970), p. 89. See entire chapter in Stuart: "Rx for Failure: Dispositional Diagnosis," pp. 65-102. Also see: Alan M. Dershowitz, "Dangerousness

as a Criterion for Confinement," *Bulletin of the American Academy of Psychiatry and the Law,* September 1974, *2*(3), 172-9.

20. *Hobson v. Hansen.* See note 12.

21. A San Francisco city school district, in 1973, operated a Guidance Service Center for troublemaking children. At one point it housed 101 students, 96 of whom were black. All twelve members of the committee which transferred students to the Center were white. Clients of other less drastic programs, such as home tutoring or placement in private schools, were predominantly white.

22. D. J. Franks, "Ethnic and Social Status Characteristics of Children in Educable Mentally Retarded and Learning Disabled Classes," *Exceptional Children,* 1971, *37,* 537-8. Blacks more often are designated EMR while whites are labeled LD, and whites are more likely to win their way back into a regular classroom.

23. *Mills v. Board of Education of District of Columbia* (see the Annotated Table of Cases).

CHAPTER THREE

1. "Policing the Family Fights," *Boston Globe,* September 25, 1974, p. 31.

2. Under the federally funded Alcohol Safety Action Program an offender faces a charge with a possible one year in jail, a fine, and loss of driver's license for six months to a year—or he can "voluntarily" enter counseling for up to a year.

3. An agreement between the District of Columbia Department of Human Resources and the National Capitol Housing Authority provides that managers of public housing are to watch for, among other things, parents who demonstrate an inability to establish acceptable

behavior within the family. Social workers are then to visit the family to analyze the situation, and develop a plan and monitor its progress on a regular basis. Families that do not cooperate with the social workers will be evicted.

4. "The right of the people to be secure in their persons, houses, papers and effects, against unreasonable searches and seizures, shall not be violated, and no Warrants shall issue, but upon probable cause, supported by oath or affirmation, and particularly describing the place to be searched, and the persons or things to be seized."

5. *McNeil v. Director, Patuxent Institution* (see the Annotated Table of Cases) suggests that the Fifth Amendment right against self-incrimination allows a refusal to cooperate in a process that may result in a deprivation of liberty. In addition there may be a Fourth Amendment right not to be observed, if diagnosis will be based on the observed behavior, when the state does not have a right to be there observing in the first place. *Narcotic Addiction Control Commission v. James*, 22 N.Y.2d. 545 (1968).

6. Chapter 1, note 9.

7. Established under Title II, Part A of the National Research Act, P.L. 93-348.

8. Where courts *do* see a conflict between parental and child interests, and where there are inadequate due process measures to safeguard the child, the court may bar an action such as a "voluntary" commitment. *Saville v. Treadway*, Civil Action No. 6969 (M.D. Tenn. March 8, 1974).

9. I am indebted for this notion to Dr. Sidney Bijou, child psychologist now at the University of Arizona and Chairman of the American Psychological Association Commission on Behavior Modification.

1. F. Gray, P. S. Graubard, and H. Rosenberg, "Little Brother is Changing You," *Psychology Today*, March 1974, 7(10), 42.

2. *Morales v. Turman* (see the Annotated Table of Cases).

3. In *Donaldson v. O'Connor* (see the Annotated Table of Cases) the defendants argued that there was treatment because the patient was allowed to interact with groups. The court found this was an attempt to leave Donaldson out of any meaningful treatment program.

4. In *Morales* the court noted that simply because there was some structuring to the environment, that did not mean treatment was occurring. The label "milieu therapy" is often used by defendants to otherwise dignify what courts find to be no treatment at all. See: J. Cumming, and E. Cumming, *Ego and Milieu: Theory and Practice of Environmental Therapy* (New York: Atherton Press, 1967).

5. R. P. Liberman, L. W. King, W. J. DeRisi, and M. McCann, *Personal Effectiveness: Guiding People to Assert Themselves and Improve Their Social Skills* (Champaign, Ill.: Research Press, 1975).

6. *New York State Association for Retarded Children v. Rockefeller* (see the Annotated Table of Cases).

7. *PARC.*

8. Experimental approaches may receive a stimulus from recent decisions on the right to treatment. "Indeed, if there are constitutional rights to treatment and rehabilitation, and if the arts of treatment and rehabilitation are in a primitive state, if there are promising potential therapies (e.g. behavior modification), and if research and development may aid patients through the development of new and better techniques, does it not follow

that courts must order that research and development programs take place?" R. G. Spece, "Conditioning and Other Techniques Used to 'Treat?' 'Rehabilitate?' 'Demolish?' Prisoners and Mental Patients." 45 So. Cal. L. Rev. 616 (1972).

9. *Defense Department CHAMPUS Programs.* Permanent Subcommittee on Investigations, Committee on Government Operations, United States Senate, Ninety-Third Congress, Second Session, July 23-26, 1974.

10. *Mackey v. Procunier* (see the Annotated Table of Cases).

11. Alan A. Stone, M.D. Dr. Stone's formal presentation, "The Right to Treatment and the Medical Establishment" (pp. 159-67), and other papers from this excellent symposium are reprinted in: *Bulletin of the American Academy of Psychiatry and the Law,* September 1974, *2*(3), 137-95.

12. Prisoners who undergo psychosurgery to cure violent behavior often remain in prison, remain violent, but also suffer other effects of brain destruction. *Memorandum on the Center for the Study of Violent Behavior.* A study prepared by the Committee Opposing Psychiatric Abuse of Prisoners, April 5, 1973. Reprinted in: *Individual Rights and the Federal Role in Behavior Modification.* A study prepared by the Staff of the Subcommittee on Constitutional Rights of the Committee on the Judiciary, United States Senate, Ninety-Third Congress, Second Session, November 1974. For an opposing view, see: V. H. Mark, "A Psychosurgeon's Case for Psychosurgery," *Psychology Today,* July 1974, *8*(2), 28.

13. Medical and psychiatric literature is filled with discussions of brain abnormality, but nowhere is evidence cited that surgery would have altered a specific behavior or that other therapies would not have worked better. See: *Quality of Health Care—Human Experimentation, 1973.* Hearings before the Subcommittee on Health,

Committee on Labor and Public Welfare, United States Senate, Ninety-Third Congress, First Session, February 23 and March 6, 1973, Part 2. The views of two major proponents of psychosurgery are elaborated in: V. H. Mark, and F. Ervin, *Violence and the Brain* (New York: Harper and Row, 1970); and legal implications of their views are analyzed in the excellent review of their book: D. Wexler, 85 Harv. L. Rev. 1489 (1972).

14. T. J. Teyler, *A Primer of Psychobiology: Brain and Behavior* (San Francisco: Freeman, 1975), pp. 114-9.

15. B. Ingraham, and G. W. Smith, "The Use of Electronics in the Observation and Control of Human Behavior and Its Possible Use in Rehabilitation and Parole," *Issues in Criminology*, 1973, 7(2), 35-53.

16. Ibid.

17. R. K. Schwitzgebel, *Development and Legal Regulation of Coercive Behavior Modification Techniques with Offenders.* NIMH Crime and Delinquency Series, February 1971. Dr. Schwitzgebel, a pioneer in the development of instrumentation in this field, is also an attorney and has written widely, pointing up the many possible problems of using his instruments. Dr. Schwitzgebel recently stated, "At the present time I'm not in favor of using this equipment because I think it would be misused." M. Casady, "The Electronic Watchdog We Shouldn't Use," *Psychology Today*, January 1975, 8(8), 84.

18. Schwitzgebel, pp. 11 and 19-21. See note 17.

19. "Attack on Electroshock," *Newsweek*, March 17, 1975, p. 86.

20. L. H. Cotter, "Operant Conditioning in a Vietnamese Mental Hospital." In: R. Ulrich, T. Stachnick, and J. Mabry (eds.), *Control of Human Behavior* (vol. 2) (Glenview, Ill.: Scott Foresman, 1970), pp. 100-5.

21. Chapter 2, note 7. See also: F. Ausubel, J. Beckwith, and K. Janssen, "The Politics of Genetic Engineering: Who Decides Who's Defective," *Psychology Today,* June 1974, *8*(1), 30.

22. *Buck v. Bell,* 274 U.S. 200 (1927).

23. Note 21.

24. B. Feingold, *Why Your Child Is Hyperactive* (New York: Random House, 1974). K. E. Moyer, "Allergy and Aggression," *Psychology Today,* July 1975, *9*(2), 76.

25. H. M. Ross, "Orthomolecular Psychiatry," *Psychology Today,* April 1974, *7*(11), 82.

26. E. M. Abrahamson, and A. W. Pazat, *Body, Mind and Sugar* (New York: Holt, 1950). S. Walker, "Blood Sugar and Emotional Storms," *Psychology Today,* July 1975, *9*(2), 69.

27. Judicial investigations into drug use in experiments, such as in *Mackey,* showed therapists exhorting subjects to change their ways.

28. E. B. Welsch, "You May Not Know It, But Your Schools Probably Are Deeply into the Potentially Dangerous Business of Teaching with Drugs," *American School Board Journal,* February 1974, 41-5. C. Witter, "Drugging and Schooling," *Trans-Action,* July-August 1971, 31.

29. *Federal Involvement in the Use of Behavior Modification Drugs on Grammar School Children of the Right to Privacy Inquiry.* See Chapter 2, note 5.

30. "Drugs No Cure in Hyperactivity," *Kansas City Times,* April 8, 1972, p. 12-A. Dr. Mark Stewart, the psychiatrist who in 1966 proclaimed that amphetamines act to quiet hyperactive children, is quoted as stating that six years' experience with the treatment indicates it is ineffective, that since symptoms are masked the real problems are

not addressed, that once the drug is discontinued the symptoms reappear, and that a drug dependency is often created.

31. The federal court in *Wyatt v. Stickney* (see the Annotated Table of Cases) indicated that ". . . medication shall not be used as punishment, for the convenience of staff, as a substitute for a program, or in quantities that interfere with the patient's treatment program" (p. 380).

32. Schwitzgebel, p. 10. See note 17.

33. Ibid, p. 11.

34. J. Mitford, *Kind and Usual Punishment: The Prison Business* (New York: Knopf, 1973), p. 128.

35. Surprisingly, behaviors such as swearing, lying, smoking, and not standing up when told to are often the targets of aversive behavior change efforts.

36. P. S. Houts, and M. Serber (eds.), *After the Turn On, What?* (Champaign, Ill.: Research Press, 1972), pp. 45-59, 123-31.

37. "Sheriff's Aide Retracts Theory," *Washington Post,* Sept. 3, 1972, p. 14. The head of the Los Angeles county Sheriff's Academy for fourteen years used what he termed a "stress" or "authoritarian" training model based on Army basic training. For his Ph.D. thesis, Howard Earle decided to prove that his system was best. After a three-year study, carefully using control groups, he proved himself wrong. "By every measurable standard, cadets given the non-stress program—friendly superiors, relaxed atmosphere, an opportunity to question and discuss their orders—far outperformed the cadets subjected to stress training." Two and a half years later the results were the same; those same "non-stress" cadets still followed orders more willingly, showed more enthusiasm for the job, conveyed a better physical appearance, and even scored higher as marksmen.

38. Reprinted in: *Individual Rights and the Federal Role in Behavior Modification.* See note 12.

39. For an example of group pressure applied democratically to foster positive goals, see: C. J. Braukman, D. L. Fixsen, K. A. Kirgin, E. A. Phillips, E. L. Phillips, and M. M. Wolf, "Achievement Place: The Training and Certification of Teaching Parents." In: W. S. Wood (ed.), *Issues in Evaluating Behavior Modification* (Champaign, Ill.: Research Press, 1975). E. L. Phillips, E. A. Phillips, D. L. Fixsen, and M. M. Wolf, *The Teaching Family Handbook* (Lawrence, Kan.: University of Kansas, 1972). D. L. Fixsen, M. M. Wolf, and E. L. Phillips, "Achievement Place: A Teaching Family Model of Community-Based Group Homes for Youth in Trouble." In: L. A. Hamerlynck, L. C. Handy, and E. J. Mash (eds.), *Behavior Change: Methodology, Concepts and Practice* (Champaign, Ill.: Research Press, 1973).

40. The School Board of Prince Georges County, Maryland has voted on several occasions to create such schools, but their establishment would require busing of students, something the board members want to avoid even more than they want to teach patriotism. They have not yet resolved their dilemma.

41. R. Martin, and D. Lauridsen, *Developing Student Discipline and Motivation* (Champaign, Ill.: Research Press, 1974), pp. 17-24.

CHAPTER FIVE

1. A current source of controversy is the question whether a behavior modifier can in fact change only behavior without changing something internal to the individual. Psychosurgery, electrical stimulation of the brain (ESB), electroshock, and drugs certainly intrude into the individual and even into the brain. But what of simple operant conditioning, in which consequences of behav-

ior are manipulated but the individual is never even touched? Critics cite several lines of attack against "behavior mod"—that it involves an impermissible tinkering with the mental processes (a standard alluded to by the *Mackey* court), an intrusion into personality the privacy of which is protected by at least the Ninth Amendment, or an interference with "mentation," the generation of ideas the expression of which is protected by the First Amendment.

An oft-cited source is *Stanley v. Georgia,* 397 U.S. 557 (1969), in which the Supreme Court stated: "Our whole constitutional heritage rebels at the thought of giving government the power to control men's minds . . . . Whatever the power of the state to control dissemination of ideas inimical to public morality, it cannot constitutionally premise legislation on the desirability of controlling a person's private thoughts."

Much of the work contributed by the Skinnerian side of behavioral psychology suggests that behavior is the product not of mind, personality, or mental processes but rather of the environment. Thus to change such behavior would neither invade the personality nor tinker with mental processes. This debate will doubtless long continue but for now the organically intrusive therapies are the only ones likely to be barred by the above line of reasoning, and goals of overt behavior change will probably be allowable.

2. Dershowitz. See Chapter 2, note 19.

3. Chapter 2, notes 21 and 22.

4. E. Goffman, *Asylums—Essays on the Social Situations of Mental Patients and Other Inmates* (Garden City, N.Y.: Anchor Books, 1961).

5. *Wyatt v. Stickney.*

6. *Souder v. Brennan* (see the Annotated Table of Cases).

7. The responses of mental institutions to *Souder* has

varied from state to state, and in some cases the effect of *Souder* has been to lessen therapy opportunities. An excellent series—"From Peonage to Pay"—indicates various state responses. *Behavior Today*, December 16, 1974, *5*(46), 331.

8. Chapter 4, note 34.

9. *Jackson v. Indiana,* 406 U.S. 715 (1972).

10. Where duration is limitless, treatment is *de facto* ineffective and cannot be allowed to simply continue. R. K. Schwitzgebel, "Implementing a Right to Effective Treatment," *Law and Psychology Review*, Spring 1975, 117-30.

11. Albert Shanker, President of the American Federation of Teachers, testifying before the Senate Subcommittee on Juvenile Delinquency, April 1975.

12. Anne Arundel Learning Center, Anne Arundel County, Maryland, is generally considered a model of this type of alternate school.

13. P. L. 92-318, Title IX, 20 U.S.C. 1681.

14. Atascadero State Mental Hospital. See: W. Sage, "Clockwork Lemon," *Human Behavior,* September 1974, 24-5.

15. Chapter 4, note 34.

16. J. V. McConnell, "Criminals Can Be Brainwashed—Now," *Psychology Today,* April 1970, *3*(10) 14-8, 74.

17. Chapter 4, note 34, pp. 123-4.

18. For example, punishing a student for criticizing school policy in a constitutionally protected exercise of free speech. I once visited schools in eighteen states for a project run by the Office of Economic Opportunity and repeatedly raised examples of students being disciplined for "offenses" that had been clearly established as permissible conduct by courts. Just as repeatedly, I was

told by principals that they would continue to punish those students.

19. L. E. Raths, M. Harmin, and S. B. Simon, *Values and Teaching* (Columbus, Ohio: Merrill, 1966).

20. P. L. 93-380 section 438. Senator Buckley's amendment would have required parental consent before any "attitude-affecting activity." Congressional Record, May 9, 1974 at S-7534, Ninety-Third Congress, Second Session.

21. *An Act concerning Education—Rights of Parents as to Curriculum and Methods of Instruction,* filed in the Senate of Maryland by Senator McGurk, November 30, 1973. Section A(5) provides: "No employee of a school, and no person brought into a school by the administration, may seek to subvert parental authority by acting as a change agent of attitudes, values and religious or political beliefs of the students." Section E(1) provides, in part, "No psychological or psychiatric methods shall be practiced in the public schools."

CHAPTER SIX

1. *Donaldson.*

2. *Morales.*

3. *New York State Association for Retarded Children.*

4. *Jordan v. Fitzharris,* 257 F.Supp. 674 (N.D. Cal. 1966).

5. *Mackey.*

6. The court in *Wyatt* provided for Human Rights Committees to oversee any use of aversive stimuli, and many states are now drafting guidelines which might bring the necessary degree of regulation to this highly controversial treatment approach.

7. The debate over whether prisons should punish or rehabilitate has heightened with statements by President

Gerald Ford and his two Attorneys General. Their consensus is that prisons should not bother with "correction" but should simply keep socially undesirable persons away from the rest of society for a time. Following their logic, there should be no behavior change programs at all in the federal prisons. Yet the National Bureau of Prisons continues in its plans for experimental treatment programs.

8. *McNeil.*

9. Chapter 4, note 5.

10. B. F. Skinner, *Beyond Freedom and Dignity* (New York: Knopf, 1971). B. F. Skinner, *About Behaviorism* (New York: Knopf, 1974).

11. Chapter 4, note 5.

12. D. Lauridsen, *A Token Economy Handbook for Schools: Procedures to Motivate Reluctant Learners.* Unpublished manuscript, 1975.

13. For a thorough analysis of problems facing token systems, see: D. B. Wexler, "Token and Taboo: Behavior Modification, Token Economies and the Law." 61 Calif. L. Rev. 81 (1973).

14. *Morales.*

15. *Wyatt* established minimum conditions for mental patients and the retarded, and *Morales* enumerated basic rights for juveniles. No single case has yet listed basic rights for prisoners, but individual cases have indicated a sense of a not-indecent environment to which a prisoner is entitled. Even without a basic level of rights, if the program involves taking certain items of personal property—such as clothing or reading material—then a different constitutional barrier, due process, is raised.

16. H. L. Cohen, and J. Filipczak, *A New Learning Environment* (San Francisco: Jossey-Bass, 1971).

17. G. R. Patterson, and E. Gullion, *Living with Children*

(Champaign, Ill.: Research Press, 1971). G. R. Patterson, *Families* (Champaign, Ill.: Research Press, 1975).

18. Ibid.

19. A federal court in Minnesota was even stricter, suggesting that a resident in seclusion must be checked every half hour. *Welsch v. Likins,* 373 F.Supp. 487 (D. Minn. 1974).

CHAPTER SEVEN

1. *Prince Georges County* (Maryland) *Sentinel,* April 25, 1973, p. 1.

2. Banneker Elementary School in Gary, Indiana was taken over by Behavioral Research Laboratories in the school year 1970-71. *Education Turnkey News,* August 1970, *1*(5), 2.

3. Under an Office of Economic Opportunity experiment in 1970-71 in forty schools in eighteen states, private companies contracted to take over the classes in reading and mathematics at grade levels 1, 2, 3, 7, 8 and 9.

4. Note 1.

5. Attorney Generals Opinion No. M-666, August 20, 1970.

CHAPTER EIGHT

1. R. Martin, "Performance Contracting: Making It Legal," *Nation's Schools,* January 1971, *87*(1), 62. R. Martin, and C. Blaschke, "Contracting for Educational Reform," *Phi Delta Kappan,* March 1971, 403-6. R. Martin, "Peformance Contracts with Teachers." A speech before the National School Board Association, April 6, 1971. R. Martin, "Performance Contracting:

Did We Learn Anything?" *American School Board Journal,* January 1972, 30-2. R. Martin, C. Blaschke, and P. Briggs, *Performance Contracting in Education* (Champaign, Ill.: Research Press, 1971).

2. Many public institutions are so bad today that no experiment could truly duplicate "actual" conditions. But the critical variables—salaries and other budget items, staff size, training, and ratio to clients—could be duplicated. What would undoubtedly be demonstrated is that alternative systems would be shown to meet institutional objectives with fewer social and economic costs.

3. R. A. Ehrle, "Performance Contracting for Human Services," *Personnel and Guidance Journal,* October 1970, *49*(2), 119-22.

4. Experience in a majority of sites under the OEO experiment (see Chapter 7, note 3) indicated this.

5. P.L. 90-247, Title VII, 20 U.S.C. 880 (b).

6. Conversations from 1971-1975 with Alfred J. Morin of Alfred J. Morin Associates, Washington, D.C. Mr. Morin's firm has probably performed more education accomplishment audits than any other single firm. See also: A. J. Morin, "Education Accomplishment Audit: Past, Present and Future." Proceedings of a National Symposium on Perspectives on the Education Audit, Ohio State University, Columbus, Ohio, May 21-23, 1973.

7. The preparation of Figures 1 and 2 was made possible with the help of my colleague in all things behavioral, David Lauridsen.

8. Chapter 1, note 7.

CHAPTER NINE

1. Materials in this chapter appeared in: R. Martin, *Behav-*

ior Modification: Human Rights and Legal Responsibilities (Champaign, Ill.: Research Press, 1974).

2. B. A. Tanner, and J. J. Parrino, *Helping Others: Behavioral Procedures for Mental Health Workers* (Eugene, Ore.: E-B Press, 1975), p. 159. Tanner and Parrino report one state hospital where psychologists set up a program in which patients were charged tokens for medication prescribed by a physician.

3. See: T. Risley, "Certify Procedures Not People." In: W. S. Wood (ed.), *Issues in Evaluating Behavior Modification* (Champaign, Ill.: Research Press, 1975).

4. In *Carter v. Carlson,* 447 F.2d. 358 (D.C. 1971), the court found the defendants had violated their duty to supervise their subordinates by failing to institute a system of training, instruction, monitoring, and discipline which would prevent, or discover and remedy, wrongful action. In *Wright v. McMann,* 460 F.2d. 126 (2nd. Cir. 1972), the court stated, "In short, applying the common law tort standard . . . that one is liable for the 'natural consequences of his actions,' we think appellant . . . knew or should have known that Wright was being forced to live under conditions described previously by this court as 'foul' and 'inhumane' and today held unconstitutional" (p. 135). Money damages were allowed against the warden because he had failed to find out and correct the wrong. In *Wood v. Strickland,* 95 S.Ct. 992 (1975), the Supreme Court stated that those in charge of a program, in this case a school board, cannot claim ignorance. They must know the basic constitutional rights of those in their charge, and they are liable for damages if they reasonably should have known that a violation of those rights was occurring.

CHAPTER TEN

1. "Early Prediction of Individual Violence." Reprinted in:

Individual Rights and the Federal Role in Behavior Modification, pp. 384-6. See Chapter 4, note 12.

2. As the Supreme Court in *Wisconsin v. Constantineau,* 400 U.S. 433 (1971), stated: "Where a person's good name, reputation, honor or integrity are at stake, because of what the government is doing to him, notice and an opportunity to be heard are essential . . . . Only when the whole proceedings leading to the pinning of an unsavory label on a person are aired can oppressive results be prevented."

3. Chapter 5, note 20.

4. In *Whitree v. New York State,* 290 N.Y.S.2d. 486 (Ct. Claims 1968), the court focused on the inadequacy of records as the reason that an inmate had been held for over twelve years in a mental hospital. "To the extent that a hospital record develops information for subsequent treatment, it contributed to the inadequate treatment this claimant received."

5. *Williams v. Robinson* (see the Annotated Table of Cases) treats a hospital as just another administrative agency and accountable for its actions as such. The court stated it would not substitute its judgment as to whether the best decision was made but would inquire into the integrity of the decision-making process. The affected individual must have been able to present evidence, and the hospital must have an administrative record which was relied on in making its decision and that record must, on its face, justify the decision. The court held flatly that rules governing judicial review of administrative agencies apply with equal force to proceedings to test the propriety of internal hospital decisions with regard to the manner of confinement and adequacy of treatment received by the patient.

6. 5 U.S.C. section 552 *et seq.*

7. *Washington Research Project, Inc. v. Department of*

Health, Education and Welfare, 366 F.Supp. 929 (D.C. 1973). The plaintiff wanted to see documents on research being conducted on drugs used to modify school childrens' behavior. The court held that descriptions of research are not confidential and that the grant decision-making process is subject to the provisions of the Freedom of Information Act. On-site visits and reports will be made public and the whole grant awarding process may well be opened up with due process guarantees to be followed in awarding or denying requests for funds.

8. *National Prison Project of American Civil Liberties Union Foundation, Inc. v. Sigler,* 390 F.Supp. 789 (D.C. 1975). In this case the parole board argued that the process by which they determine whether an individual is ready for release is not an "adjudication" as contemplated in the Administrative Procedures Act, that their actions are not formal "opinions" or "orders" which should be written down and made public, and that the Freedom of Information Act's bar against invasion of privacy would prevent disclosure. These seem to be exactly the kind of arguments that an administrator of a behavior change project would make. The federal court struck them down, arguing that the Act covers the "agency process" leading to the "final disposition" of any matter and that privacy can be protected by simply deleting identifying details.

CHAPTER ELEVEN

1. The First Amendment provides that "Congress shall make no law respecting an establishment of religion, or prohibiting the free exercise thereof; or abridging the freedom of speech or of the press; or the right of the people peaceably to assemble, and to petition the Government for a redress of grievances." In *Brown v. Schubert,* 347 F.Supp. 232 (E.D. Wis. 1972), two

patients in a mental hospital wrote letters to a local newspaper and were placed in solitary. The court found such an attempt to influence their behavior was prohibited because their action was protected by the First Amendment.

2. Chapter 1, note 3.

3. The Sixth Amendment provides for assistance of counsel in defense of criminal prosecutions, but courts have applied its protection wherever counsel is needed in a basically adversary proceeding.

4. The Eighth Amendment prohibits the infliction of "cruel and unusual punishments." See: *Burns v. Swenson,* 430 F.2d. 771 (8th Cir. 1970) and *Haines v. Kerner,* 404 U.S. 519 (1972).

5. Except with regard to prisoners, the Thirteenth Amendment prohibits "involuntary servitude." See: P. R. Friedman, "Thirteenth Amendment and Statutory Rights Concerning Work in Mental Institutions." In: B. J. Ennis, and P. R. Friedman (eds.), *Legal Rights of the Mentally Handicapped* (New York: Practicing Law Institute, 1974), pp. 273-94.

6. Chapter 1, note 5.

7. S. W. Wood (ed.), *Issues in Evaluating Behavior Modification* (Champaign, Ill.: Research Press, 1975). See, particularly, articles by Agras, Sulzer-Azaroff, Risley, Michael, and Krapfl.

8. 5 U.S.C. section 552 *et seq.*

9. Corporal punishment is still advocated by many, including the United Federation of Teachers. A 1972 task force report by the National Education Association showed "the use of strap and rod declines in direct proportion to the student's age and size." (F. M. Hechinger, and G. Hechinger, "Thou Shalt Beat Him With the Rod and Shalt Deliver His Soul from Hell," *New York Times*

Magazine, October 6, 1974, p. 26.) Obviously, corporal punishment is practiced by the strong on the weak, which raises questions about those who support it so enthusiastically. It is even advanced by one writer as the new answer to criticism of electric aversive stimuli: Don't stand around waiting to be attacked for shocking kids, beat them. (J. F. Killory, "Corporal Punishment as an Alternative to Electroshock in Aversive Psychotherapeutic Procedures with Children and Adolescents," *Behavioral Engineering,* 1975, *2*(3), 70-1.) One federal court has found it to violate the Eighth Amendment and states, "The uncontradicted evidence of the authorities suggests that the practice does not serve either as useful punishment or as treatment. Testimony adduced at the trial shows that it actually breeds counter-hostility resulting in greater aggression by a child. . . . [Corporal punishment] offends contemporary concepts of decency and human dignity and precepts of civilization which we profess to possess." (*Nelson v. Heyne,* 355 F.Supp. 451 (N.D. Ind. 1972) at 454.) If legislatures do not ban this senseless practice they should at least require due process rights during its administration. Having to accord the victim the decency of due process would probably cause perpetrators of corporal punishment to lose their taste for it.

CHAPTER TWELVE

1. L. A. Stevens, *Explorers of the Brain* (New York: Knopf, 1971).

2. R. McIntire, "Licensing Parenthood," *Psychology Today,* October 1973, *7*(5), 34. For a more voluntary approach, see: R. P. Hawkins, "It's Time We Taught the Young How to Be Good Parents (and Don't You Wish We'd Started a Long Time Ago?)" *Psychology Today,* November 1972, *6*(6), 28.

3. E. Wickenden, *Back to the Poor Law via Section 1115.* National Assembly for Social Policy and Development, New York, mimeo, May 4, 1971.

4. New York's application was entitled "Incentives for Independence" and was submitted to HEW September 9, 1971.

5. E. Wickenden, *Notes on HR 1—New York State Demonstration Projects.* National Assembly for Social Policy and Development, New York, mimeo, September 28, 1971.

Annotated Table of Cases

The following cases, while not all dealing directly with behavior change programs, affect areas of concern in this book. Many of them are currently being appealed; these should not be taken to be final or definitive statements of the law.

Clonce v. Richardson, 379 F.Supp. 338 (W.D. Mo. 1974)

The federal prison psychiatric facility at Springfield, Missouri established a behavior modification project to deal with prisoners not adjusting to the prison environment. Prisoners were involuntarily transferred into the project, known as START, for Special Training and Rehabilitative Treatment, in which they began in an environment stripped of all amenities and then worked their way up through several tiers. Attorneys for plaintiffs argued that the beginning level was really cruel and unusual punishment and that inmates were sometimes shackled to bare beds, forced to eat out of large bowls without using their hands, and not released to perform bodily functions. The Federal Bureau of Prisons discontinued the project, and the federal district court thus refused to rule on many of the points raised by the American Civil Liberties Union Fund National Prison Law Project. The case did establish that a behavior modification project which begins by depriving the person of something represents a sufficient change in status that the individuals must be accorded full due process guarantees of notice, hearing, and opportunity to contest their inclusion in the project.

Covington v. Harris, 419 F.2d. 617 (D.C. 1969)

The plaintiff was an inmate of a mental hospital and was transferred to the maximum security ward of the hospital. The Federal Court of Appeals for the District of Columbia held that whenever an alternative placement is considered, within a hospital as well as outside of an institution, the least restrictive alternative which serves the purpose of the commitment must be explored first.

Donaldson v. O'Connor, 493 F.2d. 507 (5th Cir. 1974)

Donaldson was civilly committed to a Florida mental institution. For religious reasons he refused the first two therapies offered him, electroshock and tranquilizing drugs. He was offered virtually no other type of therapy for the next fifteen years. Donaldson sued for his release claiming he had a right either to be treated or released. The Federal Court of Appeals for the Fifth Circuit held that there is a constitutional right to such individual treatment as will help the patient to be cured or to improve his mental condition. Where the justification for commitment is treatment, it violates due process if the treatment is not provided. If the justification for commitment is dangerousness to self or others, treatment is the *quid pro quo* society must pay as the price of the extra safety it derives from the denial of the individual's liberty.

Donaldson also sued for damages under a federal statute that provides that anyone acting under color of state authority who deprives a person of his constitutional rights is liable for damages. Donaldson was awarded $38,500 from the two doctors in charge of his care.

In Re Gault, 387 U.S. 1 (1967)

Gault was a fifteen-year-old sent to a state industrial school for making obscene phone calls. He complained that the juvenile hearing did not accord him full due process rights. The state argued that due process was not required because the proceedings were not of a criminal or punitive nature but rather were to benefit the youth. The Supreme Court held that the impact of the hearing—a potential loss of liberty—required that the youth receive full due process rights and that labeling the hearing "for the good of the child" did not remove its basically adversary nature. The Court's requirements for due process were that the juvenile receive notice of the charges against him, right to counsel at a hearing in which he could confront accusers and cross-examine them, right to refuse to testify against himself, right to a transcript of the hearing, and right to appeal.

Goss v. Lopez, 95 S.Ct. 729 (1975)

Several high school students suspected of being involved in a lunchroom disturbance were summarily suspended from school. The Supreme Court held that the effect of such an action was to influence the students' freedom of association and the way other students and teachers viewed them, and was thus a sufficient deprivation of liberty that the constitutional requirement—no one shall be deprived of liberty without due process of law—was raised. Due process in such cases requires at least notice and a hearing. Mr. Justice Powell, dissenting, noted that a suspension was certainly no more severe than other activities such as assigning a student to a special program. This case will thus likely serve as precedent for those claiming that assignment of a student to a behavior modification treatment program must afford notice and hearing before the transfer. Even if a student in a regular classroom is treated differently than other students (given tokens, subject to Time Out), thus altering the way others view him, it might be sufficient deprivation of liberty to raise the due process issue. Thus in any separate treatment or classification there should first be notice and a hearing to discuss the approach with the student and his parents.

Griswold v. Connecticut, 381 U.S. 479 (1965)

Plaintiffs were charged with violating Connecticut state law which prohibited anyone from aiding others in preventing conception. The plaintiffs, in their work for Planned Parenthood, regularly and publicly counseled contraception. The Supreme Court struck down the state law, arguing that personal affairs fall "within the zone of privacy created by several fundamental constitutional guarantees" and quoted the Ninth Amendment which suggests unnamed rights retained by the people. The first eight amendments to the Constitution do not exhaust all the rights guaranteed to the people and so the Ninth Amendment is construed to contain implicitly a right of privacy, a general right to be let alone. Mr. Justice Goldberg, concurring, adds the test that for the state to encroach upon this right to be let alone, there must be a compelling state interest which is directly related to the accomplishment of a permissible state policy.

Kaimowitz v. Michigan Department of Mental Health, 42 U.S.L. Week 2063 (Mich. Cir. Ct., Wayne Cty. July 10, 1973)

An involuntarily committed mental patient volunteered to undergo psychosurgery in order to cure his fits of uncontrollable aggression. The state court held that he could not consent: "Involuntarily confined mental patients live in an inherently coercive institutional environment. Indirect and subtle psychological coercion has a profound effect upon the patient population." Even if the patient were able to consent, the court indicated it would not allow the procedure because it would violate the right to privacy and the First Amendment which "protects the generation and free flow of ideas from unwarranted interference with one's mental processes."

If the *Kaimowitz* reasoning is widely adopted it might mean that behavioral approaches which are experimental, and thus require consent, may not be attempted with prisoners or mental patients who are involuntarily confined. Taking *Kaimowitz* to its logical extension, it would bar any behavioral intervention which "interfered with one's mental processes." Obviously it will be up to other courts to define these terms with more precision.

Knecht v. Gilman, 488 F.2d. 1136 (8th Cir. 1973)

Mental patients were involuntarily administered a drug to induce vomiting for up to an hour as part of an aversive behavior change program. Offenses which provoked this treat-

172

ment included swearing and not standing when told. Testimony conflicted whether "behavior modification by aversive stimuli" was an acceptable approach or whether it was an effective one. The federal appeals court noted that calling the procedure "treatment" did not insulate it from Eighth Amendment scrutiny and held that it was cruel and unusual punishment unless it was voluntary. The court would allow such treatment only after written consent with an opportunity for the patient to withdraw his consent at any time.

Lake v. Cameron, 364 F.2d. 657 (D.C. 1966)

Mrs. Lake was a senile, elderly person unable to care for herself. She was committed to a mental institution, and she protested. The Federal Court of Appeals for the District of Columbia found that she was entitled to the least restrictive alternative available and that the burden was on the state to explore and exhaust all less restrictive alternatives before they ended up with confinement. The majority opinion stated that "Deprivations of liberty . . . should not go beyond what is necessary for [the ill person's] protection," and Judge Wright, concurring, added that the government could not involuntarily confine a person simply because he needs care. The government is not entitled "to compel Mrs. Lake to accept its help at the price of her freedom."

Lessard v. Schmidt, 349 F.Supp. 1078 (E.D. Wis. 1972)

Miss Lessard was picked up in front of her house by two police officers and taken to a mental institution for "emergency detention for mental observation." She was held for nearly a month during which time she was examined by psychiatrists, and her period of detention was lengthened several times. She was never told what was being done. The federal district court found that procedure unconstitutional and required that before a psychiatric interview notice be given that the individual has a right not to speak and that if he does speak his statements may form the basis for commitment.

The court also found that involuntary hospitalization

for observation was far too drastic, and established that a person cannot be deprived of his liberty if there are less drastic means of achieving the same goal. The court required that whoever proposes the specific treatment alternative must first show "(1) what alternatives are available; (2) what alternatives were investigated; and (3) why the investigated alternatives were not deemed suitable."

McNeil v. Director, Patuxent Institution, 407 U.S. 245 (1972)

The plaintiff was sentenced to five years for assault and was referred to the defendant institution to determine if he needed psychiatric treatment. He refused to cooperate and be examined. After five years had expired, the state proposed to keep him indefinitely until he cooperated with the examining psychiatrist. The Supreme Court said the institution had lost its right to access to the individual and could not force a psychiatric examination. Mr. Justice Douglas, concurring, added that the individual had a constitutional right to refuse to cooperate. The Fifth Amendment privilege against self-incrimination applies whenever the result of the inquiry might be a deprivation of liberty.

Mackey v. Procunier, 477 F.2d. 877 (9th Cir. 1973)

The plaintiff was an inmate at California's Vacaville prison where he claims he was involuntarily administered a suffocating drug as part of the prison staff's experiments with how aversive treatment might affect behavior. The prisoner admitted he had consented to electroshock but not to the drug. The federal appeals court sent the case back for trial stating that if the charges were proved true then it would raise "serious constitutional questions respecting cruel and unusual punishment or impermissible tinkering with the mental processes."

Mills v. Board of Education of District of Columbia, 348 F.Supp. 866 (D.C. 1972)

Approximately 12,000 students labeled mentally retarded, emotionally disturbed, physically handicapped, hyper-active, or behaviorally disordered were suspended, expelled, or transferred, or otherwise excluded from public education in the District of Columbia. The federal district court held that all school age children are entitled to public education and that they should be assigned to regular public classrooms. They could be reassigned to other educational services only if the alternative is more suited to their educational needs and only after notice and a hearing to challenge the reassignment.

Morales v. Turman, 383 F.Supp. 53 (E.D. Tex. 1974)

This case extends the right to treatment to juveniles. Several youths in the Texas juvenile justice system complained that the only justification for their incarceration was to be rehabilitated and that since treatment was nonexistent they must be released. The federal district court went farther than most courts in defining what treatment requires. Basically that includes an actual treatment program geared to the individual: "It is not sufficient for defendants to contend that merely removing a child from his environment and placing him in a 'structured' situation constitutes constitutionally adequate treatment . . . . Nor do the Texas Youth Centers' sporadic attempts at . . . 'behavior modification' through the use of point systems rise to the dignity of professional treatment programs geared to individual juveniles." Treatment also requires adequately trained and supervised staff. The court suggested that placing juveniles in unsupervised hands of unsuitable staff may be cruel and unusual punishment. The court suggested that many of the treatment techniques were sufficient deprivations of liberty that they required due process before being attempted. However, it noted that some behavior modification techniques, such as Time Out for less than one hour, are slight enough deprivations that they do not require due process procedures.

New York State Association for Retarded Children v. Rockefeller, 357 F.Supp. 752 (E.D.N.Y. 1973)

Plaintiffs were residents of a New York institution for

the mentally retarded. Several had a worse condition than before they entered the program. The federal district court said that there were a variety of standards that were used by courts—"tolerable living environment," "protection from fellow inmates or staff," and so forth—but that taken together there was definitely a constitutional right to protection from deterioration.

Pennsylvania Association for Retarded Children v. Commonwealth of Pennsylvania, 334 F.Supp. 1257 (E.D. Pa. 1971)

Thousands of school age children in Pennsylvania were excluded from school under a state law that allowed exclusion if a child were unable to benefit from education. The federal court found that all children, no matter how retarded, can benefit from a program of education and training. The state could thus no longer deny retarded children access to free public education. The state agreed in a consent decree to place children in programs appropriate to the child's capacity, with placement in a regular classroom preferable to a special class and a special class preferable to any other type of institutional placement. Educational assignments had to follow due process and must be re-evaluated every two years with notice and a hearing.

Rouse v. Cameron, 373 F.2d. 451 (D.C. 1966)

Rouse was acquitted of a criminal charge by reason of insanity and pursuant to statute was committed to a mental institution. He sought his release on grounds that he was receiving no treatment. In this case, the genesis of the right to treatment cases, the federal appeals court relied on a District of Columbia statute to hold that there is a right to either treatment or release. The court stated that ". . . involuntary confinement without treatment is shocking," and laid the groundwork for later cases which base their claims on a general constitutional right.

Souder v. Brennan, 367 F.Supp. 808 (D.C. 1973)

Eugene Souder has been in an institution for the retarded for over thirty years. He worked in the kitchen seven days a week. Five days each week he worked eleven hours a day. On the other two days he worked five and one-half hours in the morning, then four hours at other assignments, and often returned to work in the kitchen for the evening shift. He was paid two dollars a month and received two days a month off. This case forced the Department of Labor to enforce amendments to the Fair Labor Standards Act which require that minimum wages be paid for such work. Where the work assignment is clearly more in the nature of institutional maintenance than therapy, and where the institution receives the economic benefit from the work, the minimum wage must be paid.

Williams v. Robinson, 432 F.2d. 637 (D.C. 1970)

This case treats a hospital as just another administrative agency, and accountable for its actions as such. The plaintiff contested his transfer to a maximum security ward of a mental hospital claiming it was based on inaccurate information and that the decision did not consider less restrictive alternatives. The Federal Court of Appeals for the District of Columbia indicated it would not substitute its judgment as to whether the best decision was made but would inquire as to the integrity of the decision-making process. For that process to be adequate, the plaintiff must have been able to present evidence, and the hospital must have an administrative record which was relied on in making the decision and which, on its face, would justify the decision. The hospital argued that it was not an administrative agency, and that its methods of operation were not open to judicial scrutiny, but the court held that rules governing judicial review of administrative agencies apply with equal force to proceedings to test the propriety of internal hospital decisions with regard to the manner of confinement and adequacy of treatment.

Wyatt v. Stickney, 344 F.Supp. 373, 344 F.Supp. 387 (M.D. Ala. 1972) aff'd *sub nom. Wyatt v. Aderholt,* 503 F.2d. 1305 (5th Cir. 1974)

A cut in the Alabama cigarette tax led to the firing of ninety-nine employees in facilities for the mentally ill. A complaint that adequate care could not thus be maintained eventually added additional defendants and embraced three state facilities for the mentally ill and retarded. The federal district court, affirmed by the Fifth Circuit Court of Appeals, held that there was a constitutional right to adequate care. The state of Alabama argued that the notion of treatment presents questions not susceptible to judicially manageable or ascertainable standards. The court held that it could determine whether care was adequate and could formulate workable institution-wide standards.

The court focused on three fundamental conditions for effective and adequate treatment: a humane physical and psychological environment, qualified staff in numbers sufficient to administer adequate treatment, and individualized treatment plans. The court enumerated many rights which must be met. Among them are: A right to the least restrictive conditions necessary for treatment. The right to be free from isolation (with one hour as the time limit on therapeutically justifiable isolation). A right not to be subjected to experimental research without consent (with Human Rights Committees formed to approve any experimentation). A right not to be subjected to treatment procedures such as lobotomy, electroconvulsive treatment, adversive (sic) reinforcement conditioning, or other unusual or hazardous treatment procedures without express and informed consent after consultation with counsel. The right to keep and use personal possessions. The right not to be required to perform institutional maintenance work, and to receive the minimum wage if they volunteer for such work; residents may be required to perform personal housekeeping tasks and may be required to perform therapeutic work tasks if those tasks do not involve the operation or maintenance of the institution. A right to a comfortable bed and privacy. The right to access to a day room with television and other recreational facilities. The right to adequate meals—the denial of an adequate diet shall not be used as punishment. The right to adequate staff. The right to an individualized treatment plan with a projected timetable for meeting specific goals, criteria for release to less restrictive treatment conditions, and criteria for discharge.

In specific reference to behavior modification, the court stated: "No resident shall be subjected to a behavior modification program designed to eliminate a particular pattern of behavior without prior certification by a physician that he has examined the resident in regard to behavior to be extinguished and finds that such behavior is not caused by a physical condition which could be corrected by appropriate medical procedures. No resident shall be subjected to a behavior modification program which attempts to extinguish socially appropriate behavior or to develop new behavior patterns when such behavior modifications serve only institutional convenience."